*Professional Communities
and the Work of High School Teaching*

PROFESSIONAL COMMUNITIES
and the Work of High School Teaching

Milbrey W. McLaughlin and Joan E. Talbert

The University of Chicago Press Chicago and London

Milbrey W. McLaughlin is the David Jacks Professor of Education and Public Policy and **Joan E. Talbert** is a senior research scholar at Stanford University, where they codirect the Center for Research on the Context of Teaching. With David Cohen, they are coauthors of *Teaching For Understanding*.

The University of Chicago Press, Chicago 60637
The University of Chicago Press, Ltd., London
© 2001 by The University of Chicago
All rights reserved. Published 2001
Printed in the United States of America
10 9 8 7 6 5 4 3 2 1   5 4 3 2 1

ISBN (cloth): 0-226-50070-5
ISBN (paper): 0-226-50071-3

Library of Congress Cataloging-in-Publication Data

McLaughlin, Milbrey Wallin.
    Professional communities and the work of high school teaching / Milbrey
W. McLaughlin and Joan E. Talbert.
        p.   cm.
    Includes bibliographical references and index.
    ISBN 0-226-50070-5 (cloth : alk. paper) — ISBN 0-226-50071-3 (pbk. : alk. paper)
    1. High school teaching—United States.   2. Education, Secondary—Social
aspects—United States.   3. Educational change—United States.   I. Talbert,
Joan E.   II. Title.
LB1607.5 .M35   2001
373.1102—dc21

                                                                    2001001173

CONTENTS

ILLUSTRATIONS

ACKNOWLEDGMENTS

This book represents the effort, energy, and thinking of a research community that has evolved over a period of years. In 1987, the Center for Research on the Context of Teaching (CRC) was founded at Stanford University by a national grant from the U.S. Department of Education's Office of Educational Research and Improvement. The roots of our current community go back to that grant and to Elizabeth Demarest, our project monitor and a chief architect of the federal government's request for such a center. Betty was convinced that systematic inquiry into the ill-defined question of "context" would yield insights and perspectives that could contribute to improved teaching and learning.

The pages of this book announce our primary debt to the teachers, students, principals, and district officials whose experiences and reflections ground our efforts to realize the CRC's mission. Hundreds of teachers contributed precious time and energy to telling us about their work in the California and Michigan high schools we followed over four years; many invited us into their classrooms to observe and discuss their teaching practice. Teachers' and students' enthusiasms, frustrations, and insights into their work in particular school settings taught us how context matters for the quality of high school teaching and learning.

A first generation of CRC research assistants carried out field research in these schools and classrooms and helped to make sense of teachers' and students' worlds within them. They also worked with survey data to construct bridges between quantitative and qualitative perspectives on the work of high school teaching. Participants in this initial CRC community include Susan Arbuckle, Nina Bascia, Hanh Cao Yu, Allan Cook, Ann Locke Davidson, Marian Eaton, Michele Ennis, Stephen Fletcher, Jan Kerkhoven, Joseph Kahne, Jennifer Knudsen, Daniel Perlstein, Rebecca Perry, Judi Powell, Hilary Saner, Leslie Siskin, Shu-er Christina Tsai, and Choya Wilson at Stanford; Susan Threatt and Susan Sather at the University of California, Berkeley; and Yuk Fai Cheong, Sang Jin Kang, Jim Meade, Barbara Reinken, Kathleen Sernak, and James Spillane at Michigan State University.

The research upon which this book stands also reflects the imagination and active involvement of several colleagues at Stanford and elsewhere. Patricia Phelan led the research on students' experiences in the schools and classes we studied; Richard Snow's work on student tests used in national high school surveys occasioned a lively discussion concerning our field-based findings. Richard Elmore, Pam Grossman, Judith Warren Little, Steven Raudenbush, Brian Rowen, and Susan Stodolsky took responsibility for distinct lines of analysis around context questions. Their work suffuses this book and the intellectual character of the community of practice that produced it.

Our efforts to understand the contexts that matter for teaching and learning were informed, energized, and supported by members of the National Advisory Board to our OERI research center: Harry Handler, Donald Hill, Ann Lieberman, Arthur Powell, and Theodore Sizer. Their contributions to the CRC's research and thinking were fundamental and continue even though their last formal meeting was some years ago.

The community of practice that has developed around the CRC's work since the OERI grant ended, and that informs our thinking in this book, is broad and varied. It includes the students and colleagues who have been active participants in elaborating initial CRC research on the work of high school teaching and school reform more generally. A second generation of CRC research assistants and project associates have brought new questions, perspectives, and interests to our research community, enriching our understandings and generating new ways of seeing problems addressed by this book. They include Betty Achinstein, Patricia Burch, Cynthia Coburn, Ginger Cook, Linda Friedrich, JoAnn Lieberman, Teresa McCaffrey,

Ellen Meyer, Dana Mitra, Kay Moffett, Ida Oberman, Stacey Pelika, Nancy Sato, Laura Stokes, and Marjorie Wechsler.

Our ongoing research has been supported by grants from multiple sources: the National Science Foundation, the DeWitt Wallace–Reader's Digest Foundation, the Mellon and Russell Sage Foundations, the Los Angeles Educational Partnership, the Hewlett Foundation, the Stuart Foundation, and the Johnston Foundation. We are grateful for this support and its contributions to our evolving understandings of the work of high school teaching.

Several individuals have been essential resources to this book. Julie Cummer, the CRC's project administrator over many years, juggled an array of roles with expertise and good humor. Julie managed aspects of production, but more important, she provided a resource for everyone struggling to navigate Stanford accounting, travel services, and all of the day-to-day details of a research project that can frustrate and derail efforts. Janet Rutherford and Andrea Harrison have been talented and gracious assistants with all of the details involved in preparing a manuscript. Cynthia Patrick provided expert editorial assistance and an unerring eye for "educationese" and other distractions.

We are indebted to the generous colleagues who have read more versions of this manuscript that we'd care to admit. David Cohen, Michael Copland, Larry Cuban, Faith Dunne, Robert Floden, Pamela Grossman, Judith Warren Little, Ann Lieberman, Jennifer O'Day, Leslie Siskin, Richard Snow, Susan Stodolsky, and David Tyack provided extraordinarily thoughtful and helpful comment; their good advice pervades this book. Two anonymous reviewers also will see their fingerprints on the pages that follow.

John Tryneski, our University of Chicago Press editor, made the phone call that initiated this project. John has been supportive through all of the revisions and slips in schedules since that first conversation.

The colleagueship that has produced this book has been extraordinary—from the educators who welcomed us into their schools and districts, to the graduate students who interviewed, surveyed, coded, and analyzed, to the collaborators who have journeyed with us. We hope that the book captures the wisdom of our broad professional community and that it will make a difference for the work of high school teaching.

CHAPTER 1

Introduction:
Contexts of High School Teaching

Reformers and educators may not find much to agree about on topics such as school vouchers, charters, reading and math approaches, accountability strategies, or standards-based reforms, but they do agree on one point: high school practice has been and continues to be profoundly resistant to change. Yet the warrant for high school reform has never been more urgent. That venerable battleship, the public high school, today enrolls a more academically and culturally diverse student population than ever before in the nation's history. Many American teachers at all levels confront a Noah's Ark of students in terms of the variety of cultures, languages, social and economic resources, and academic skills their students bring to school. All teachers are challenged to address diverse student learning needs with limited resources. Yet as academic inequalities widen and poor students who once dropped out now stay, high school teachers face the greatest challenge. How shall they teach to "high standards for all students" when, within a single grade, reading or math levels might range from third-grade to college level? How can they succeed with the paucity of high school level materials for English language learners?

At the same time, high school teachers' task of preparing students for a productive place in society has never been more demanding. The workforce that students will enter increasingly requires not only basic literacy and numeracy, but also problem-solving skills and the capacity to continue learning as technology and society changes. Jobs have become less routine, with a steady decline in blue-collar jobs to about 10 percent and a dramatic recent increase in high-skill jobs. At the turn of this century, nearly half of all jobs require a high level of education. Further, wage disparities between high school and college graduates bring pressure on schools and teachers to prepare all students for cognitively demanding futures in higher education and work.

This book is about teachers' professional communities in American high schools at the end of the twentieth century and the striking differences in their response to the challenges of teaching. We describe how the work of teaching differed—in classroom practice, in colleague relations, and in experienced careers—across three distinct types of communities we found in the high schools and subject departments we studied during the early 1990s. We feature several schools and departments that stand out as exemplars of professional community types, showing how teachers constructed radically different professional lives within the same system and community contexts.

In considering the challenges of teaching in this era, we describe how teachers' alternative responses to contemporary students were linked to the distinctive professional cultures of their high schools or subject departments. Teachers in most high schools were left "on their own" to practice as they chose, in keeping with norms of professional autonomy in American education. However, in several high schools and departments we studied, teachers worked together in communities of practice united around shared beliefs and responsibility for teaching. These strong communities reflected two distinct cultures: in one, teachers organized to sort their increasingly diverse students into courses ranked by depth and difficulty of academic content; in another, teachers collaborated to engage all of their students in deeper conceptual understandings of subject matter.

The strong professional communities in which teachers worked together to improve their classroom practice frame our analysis of high school teaching. We pull these "teacher learning communities" onto center stage in our considerations of school contexts and policy strategies to enhance the teaching profession and public education.

We came to a focus on professional communities as a critical context of high school teaching over the course of a research program that began in fall 1988 when we first walked corridors and sat in classrooms of sixteen California and Michigan high schools. We and our colleagues of the Center for Research on the Context of Secondary School Teaching (CRC) took up a broad question: How do the various contexts of secondary schooling affect teachers' work lives and professional practice? We refined this question many times during our multiyear research program as we learned from teachers what counted in their work lives.

Our research aimed to understand the problems, and the potentials, of improving high school teaching by taking the perspective of teachers who were grappling with the challenges of preparing their students for lives in the twenty-first century. We wanted to learn how high school teachers constructed their classroom practices across the varied high school contexts in our sample and, especially, to understand what made a difference for teachers' success with nontraditional students.

This focus shaped our inquiry in a number of ways. We attended mainly to teachers' experiences of their work and profession, rather than to the formal organizational conditions of schools and the policy system with which much social science research in education was concerned at the time our study began. In keeping with research practice in occupational sociology—such as Willard Waller's (1932) and Dan Lortie's (1975) classic studies of the teaching occupation—we looked for patterns in teachers' work and careers that would reveal the profession's culture. Further, through grounded analysis of teachers' work, we sought to inform education policy from the bottom, or the inside, of the system—asking not how school sector or size or reform policy affects teaching, but what contexts matter for teachers and teaching. For this inquiry, we used a multidiscipline, multitheory lens through which to view teaching in context—or context in teaching—and in order to make sense for social science and policy of teachers' perspectives and experiences (see appendix A for a discussion of this research strategy).

High schools are organizationally and institutionally complex places to teach and to do research. The typical comprehensive high school draws around twelve hundred students from geographically and sometimes socioeconomically diverse neighborhoods, houses teachers in several academic and nonacademic subject departments, and organizes the day into a series of classes often lasting no more than fifty minutes. In general, high school teachers are assigned to teach courses in a particular subject, and their professional backgrounds and identities are linked to disciplines. Further, their locus between grade school and higher education means that high school teachers and teaching are open to a wider range of institutional influences than are their elementary or middle school counterparts. In chapter 6, we reflect on the "high schoolness" of our findings— how challenges particular to high school teaching underlie the differences in culture we found across strong professional communities—and we consider implications of our findings for practice and policy.

CONSIDERING SCHOOL CONTEXT: SOCIAL SCIENCE PERSPECTIVES AND RESEARCH DESIGN

Several prominent lines of research and theory guided our research design and inquiry into high school teachers' work lives. Social scientists' views about important contexts of teaching differ widely. Some researchers have considered the significance of school organization. Philip Jackson (1968) described ways in which the typical "egg crate" structure of schools and common features of classrooms influence how teachers see their work, for example. Researchers in the "effective schools" tradition, such as Ronald Edmonds (1979), identified strong school leadership and a clear sense of school purpose as distinguishing features of schools with strong academic records. Comparing students' experiences in public and private schools, James Coleman and Thomas Hoffer (1987) pointed to school community and strength of social ties as key conditions of effective education practice.

Other researchers have focused on education governance and policy as critical contexts of teachers' work. Susan Rosenholtz (1989) distinguished between "stuck" and "moving" district contexts and documented consequences for school coherence and teacher commitment. John Chubb and Terry Moe (1990) argued that the private school sector frees teachers from the bureaucratic constraints of public education, enabling them to be more responsive to parents and students. A similar argument comes from critical theorists such as Michael Apple (1982) and Linda McNeil (1986) who described bureaucratic controls in education as constraining teachers' professional authority and routinizing their work. Other views on how education policy systems affect teaching come from policy analysts and reformers who have examined professionalizing strategies such as new pay structures, preservice programs, and credential procedures and standards-based reform strategies that aim to increase coherence in frameworks for curriculum and accountability to stimulate and support improvement in teachers' practices.[1]

Institutional theorists have looked outside schools and policy systems for critical contexts of teaching. John Meyer and Brian Rowan's classic 1977 article argued that schools are "loosely coupled" organizations whose structures mirror rational organization and protect teachers' professional autonomy. Their work has called attention to the institutional environment as a cultural context and source of logic for what goes on in schooling. Research on social class contexts of teaching employs this lens. Jean Anyon (1980), for example, showed how English instruction differs according to the social class culture and expected student futures of schools' communities; Mary Metz (1978) documented differences in the professional cultures of schools with different social class contexts. James Rosenbaum (1976) and Jeannie Oakes (1985) showed how social class inequalities and curricular tracking within secondary schools also shape what and how teachers teach.

This research directed our attention to alternative kinds of teaching environments and conditions. We selected a large field sample of school settings that captured the contrasts of context that social scientists have argued affect teachers' work lives. We constructed a nested sixteen-school sample of states with contrasting policy systems (California leading the nation in standards-based reforms in the late 1980s and Michigan still highly decentralized); districts within each state with contrasting demographics and, in California, administrative cultures; schools that represented the range of social class and race-ethnic diversity within and between the districts. To obtain contrasts in school sector, we sampled three California independent schools with distinctive student populations and one Michigan alternative school at the margins of the public school system. The nested sample captured the multiple state, regional, district, and school contexts in which teachers' work is embedded. (See table 1.1 and appendix B for a description of the sixteen-school sample. Note that school pseudonyms are used throughout the book.)

Our research team spent four years in each of the sixteen California and Michigan schools documenting teachers' work and perceptions of context through observations, interviews, and surveys. We looked within subject departments and classrooms to uncover patterns of high school teaching within, as well as across, the schools in our sample. Our initial school visits and interviews with teachers soon revealed two contexts of teaching that depart significantly from the organizational, policy system and institutional contexts that social scientists emphasized: students and subject disciplines.

SEEING CONTEXT THROUGH TEACHERS' EYES: STUDENTS AND SUBJECTS

High school teachers told us that their students are the critical context for their teaching—that who comes to school ultimately frames their classroom tasks and experiences of success. This view resonates with others' observations that teachers often describe their work and see their professional rewards in terms of their relationships with students.[2] Teachers themselves have written that students' behavior and accomplishments affirm or destroy their self-image.[3] Jennifer Nias puts it succinctly: students function as teachers' ultimate "reality definers" (Nias 1989, 55).

Complicating the general importance of students as the context for their work and professional identity, most teachers we interviewed stressed the many ways in which "today's students" differ from "yesterday's." The majority of the teachers in our study portray yesterday's high school students as ambitious, respectful, academically talented, and supported from home. Yes-

Table 1.1 School Sample Characteristics

State/District/ School	School Type	Metro Status	Size[a]	Minority Students[b]	Poor Students[c]
California					
Mostaza District/ Region					
Scholastic	Public	Urban	S	H	M
Esperanza	Public	Urban	L	M	M
Rancho	Public	Urban	L	M	M
Greenfield	Private alt.	Suburban	S	L	L
Paloma	Private	Suburban	S	L	L
Adobe Viejo District/Region					
Valley	Public	Urban	M	M	M
Onyx Ridge	Public	Urban	M	M	M
Ibsen	Public	Urban	M	M	M
Juliet Wright	Private	Urban	S	L	L
Oak Valley District					
Oak Valley	Public	Suburban	XL	L	L
Michigan					
Burton District					
Highlander	Public	Urban	XL	H	M
Washington Academy	Public	Urban	L	H	M
Dover District					
Dover	Public	Suburban	L	L	L
Falls Park District					
LaSalle	Public	Urban	M	M	M
Monroe	Public	Urban	S	M	H
Oneida District					
Prospect	Public alt.	Suburban	S	n.a.	n.a.

[a] Sizes are reported in ranges based on the school's student enrollment at the time the sample was drawn (1988–1989): S = <885; M = 885–1500; L = 1,501–2,075; XL = >2,075.
[b] Percentage of students who are nonwhite or Hispanic: L = 0–33; M = 34–67; H = 68–100.
[c] Percentage of students who are eligible for free or reduced-price meals program: L = <10; M = 10–40; H = >40.

terday's students are remembered primarily as high achievers who comported themselves in line with expectations and who aimed at mainstream futures. Teachers' published journals echo the nostalgic accounts we heard. For example, one veteran high school teacher wrote, "What made us so good? During the olden times, and in the post-mortems that still continue, most of us thought we knew. We had a bright, ambitious, hard-working student body drawn from a stable, upper-middle-class neighborhood" (Natkins 1986, 2).

We heard such comments in most comprehensive high schools, where demographic shifts or student assignment policies, such as busing orders or transfers to newly built campuses, had altered the complexion and socioeconomic status of the student body. A number of teachers recalled the "good old days" when they had "good" students and, as one said, "teachers could teach." Two-thirds of public school teachers we surveyed reported that the students in their classes were "less prepared" than students they had taught in previous years.

Some say these views reflect only nostalgia for a "golden age" that never was (Cuban 1990). Nonetheless, America's public schools historically have been organized to educate children and youth from stable, mainstream families—students who are amply supported by family and community social and educational resources (Grubb 1995). Our country's public schools have been most successful with these "traditional" students. Students who depart in one or another respect from traditional expectations often have been labeled as "problem pupils," misfits, delinquents, or worse (Deschenes, Cuban, and Tyack, forthcoming). Moreover, in an earlier era, most "nontraditional" youth dropped out of school before or soon after entering high school; today's dropout rate is the lowest in the country's history.

The issues the teachers in our study raised about today's students largely reflect the disparities Norton Grubb (1995) and others have noted between the assumptions underlying American public schools and the realities of the youth they enroll. Teachers experience today's students as changed in nearly every respect related to and predictive of academic success—family support, consistent attendance, attention to schoolwork, and social class and language compatible with school culture.

Teachers' experience of changing student populations was especially salient in the California urban districts we studied, where high levels of immigration and desegregation policies have rapidly transformed the social, linguistic, racial, and academic composition of schools and classrooms. Most California public school teachers we talked with felt overwhelmed by the increasing diversity of learners in their classrooms. Dramatic changes in the student contexts of teaching challenged classroom routines that assumed common academic and linguistic knowledge and skills and had a profound impact on teachers' conception of their work, particularly among the two-thirds majority of urban teachers who entered the profession before 1970.

High school teachers also take their subject context as primary to their work and professional identity. The subject *matters,* as Susan Stodolsky (1988) put it; discipline cultures carry different assumptions about the nature of subject matter, student learning, and good teaching. High school teachers in our sample spoke of their subject area and particular courses within it as having classroom goals, standards for how to teach, and more or less prescribed content.

Although sociological analyses of teaching generally have treated subject areas as essentially interchangeable (Waller 1932; Jackson 1968; Rosenholtz 1989), a growing body of research describes the subjects as distinct and important contexts for teachers' interactions with students and for their professional careers.[4] Subject areas, representing as they do commitment to a discipline in college and preparation for a teaching career, significantly define the professional identities of secondary school teachers. Subjects also define organizational boundaries in typical comprehensive high schools and serve as a primary context for collegiality and shared departmental responsibility.

High school teachers referred to their particular disciplines at some point in almost every interview. They talked about ways in which their teaching depended on what their colleagues were doing in their classrooms, and about how district or state policies affected their subjects. Academic disciplines are core organizing contexts also for policy systems and thus are channels through which teaching resources and professional development opportunities flow to teachers and classrooms. Moreover, the various professional environments of teaching—in higher education, national teacher associations, local teacher networks and workshops—affect high school teachers and teaching mainly through subject channels.

Although teachers seldom mentioned new state or national standards for education regarding their individual subjects, the California frameworks were part of the context of teaching in each of the core academic subjects during the time of our study.

California teachers' experience with ambitious state standards for subject instruction provides a window into the future of the national standards movement that gained momentum during the 1990s.[5] California teachers worked in a state policy environment very different from their Michigan counterparts. It is not by happenstance that the public school teacher learning communities we found grew in the California context and not in Michigan's, as we elaborate in chapter 5.

LOOKING INTO PROFESSIONAL COMMUNITIES AND THE WORK OF HIGH SCHOOL TEACHERS

Our inquiry into patterns of classroom practice—differences in how teachers perceived and worked with students and subject matter in their classes—highlights the role that school and department professional communities can play in establishing norms for teaching. Certainly, most high school teachers worked in the kind of weak communities featured in most research on the teaching profession, in which teachers "passed like ships in the night," as one science teacher put it. Teachers' work was private and their practice highly variable in such communities. Success with students was considered a matter of individual teacher quality and student background, rather than an issue for department or school policy or collective work. Where a common pattern of practice characterized a department or school, we focused on the community's culture—the beliefs teachers shared, how they organized their work, and what meanings they made of their teaching careers. Through this inquiry, we discovered that within strong school and department communities particular, alternative teaching practices and career patterns had evolved and were sustained.

Strong professional communities establish distinctive expectations for teachers' work and interactions with students. Some strong department communities we observed developed elaborate policies for testing their students and sorting them into course sequences and achievement levels. These professional communities enforced "traditional" methods of teaching, and teachers worked to transmit predetermined course material and to administer department tests that placed students in subsequent courses. In contrast, teachers in other strong department and school communities, centered their work on students and shared responsibility for students' mastery of content and progress in the curriculum. They developed "innovative" methods of instruction that achieved a better "fit" of course work to students without compromising expectations for students' conceptual learning. Subject matter in these school or department contexts was not seen as "given" but rather as material to be reviewed and revised based on the needs and academic accomplishments of their particular students. We have come to regard the two contrasting cultures of the strong high school communities we found as reflecting cultural discontinuities and tensions in American education. While rare in the early 1990s, these communities appear now to signal divisions in secondary education that are deepening in the twenty-first century.[6]

We also look at how teaching conditions in California in the 1980s and 1990s were important in engendering movement toward strong teacher communities of practice. In terms of our sample, with the exception of the alternative Michigan school, all of the strong professional communities in public high schools were located in California. Perhaps it was a combination of jolts to their teaching routines that moved these California teachers to come together to formulate a response. By the early 1990s, they had experienced more rapid and challenging changes in student populations than had their Michigan counterparts. Their students' language diversity was extraordinary, as was cross-cutting inequality in academic preparation for high school subjects. Furthermore, state and national standards for education in core subjects challenged teachers to establish high expectations for learning outcomes. The strong California teacher communities responded differently to these challenges—some organizing around strong traditions, others innovating in their practice.

At the same time, California's curriculum and teaching frameworks in core subjects offered knowledge resources to innovative teacher communities—providing road maps of subject content through which to guide diverse learners, even when district-adopted texts seemed too inaccessible to students. The districts we studied also had begun to develop materials and professional development opportunities for teachers to enable them to help their students meet subject standards; many teachers in the innovative communities of practice we found were leaders of professional development in their districts. And beyond system boundaries, the local professional networks in the California regions offered resources of all sorts for teachers working to improve their practice—some were funded by the state, others by national and federal agencies, others through local initiatives. Both because of the challenges and jolts to teaching practice and the resources available for teacher learning, conditions in California during the early 1990s engendered stronger professional communities than are typically found in American high schools. We pick up this theme again in the chapter 6.

≈≈≈

Today's challenges to high school teaching engage key facets of classroom practice—students, content, and teaching roles. Many teachers struggle daily to address unprecedented student diversity and the widening gap between students' academic histories and their grade-level curriculum. Standards for high school instruction frame both subject content and expectations of student performance in ways that qualitatively exceed traditional goals and curriculum guides and challenge traditions of classroom practice.

Each challenge to high school teaching practice tests the profession's ability to respond in ways that support students' learning. Each challenge also presents impetus and opportunity for teachers to rethink their classroom practice and role in professional communities. How teachers respond to the incredibly diverse student populations in their schools and classrooms and how teacher communities matter for their response are core themes of our analysis.

This look into professional communities of high school teaching hopes to inform educators and others who think about prospects for improving teaching and learning in U.S. high schools. Seeing teacher community as a primary unit for improving education quality has wide-ranging implications for professional practice and for policy.

CHAPTER 2

High School Teachers' Classroom Practice

A Michigan math teacher describes his classroom dilemma this way:

> These curriculum plans were written for people who are pass-
> ing. I can do chapters 1, 2, and chapter 5 on time if everyone is
> geared up. But I've got Peggy Sue over there who's not going
> to do anything on time. I can't very well forget her and go on.
> I guess the question is: Do I follow the guidelines or do I teach
> Peggy Sue?

CHALLENGES TO TEACHING ROUTINES

What do I teach Peggy Sue? *How* do I teach Peggy Sue? Most high school teachers raised such questions when they talked with us about their practice. Peggy Sue and many of her peers challenge teachers' expectations about students and strain traditional classroom routines. Contemporary students depart in many ways from often idealized notions of the "good" student whose attitudes about school and classroom role could more or less be assumed. Today's students bring different levels of support, preparation, interests, and different academic and social needs to the classroom.

Who is the "good student" teachers cite as their marker of expected student attitudes and behavior? Ryan Moore, a high-achieving student in one of the high schools we studied, is one. Ryan's teachers describe him as "a wonderful young man. . . . Wonderful leadership skills, very responsible, highly focused . . . self-motivated, self-directed . . . much respected by his teachers . . . he just stands out. And his parents are very active here in school." Ryan's teachers, in fact, call him and his parents "ideal": "These are parents who know what their kids need and how to get it."[1]

Ryan Moore may represent an ideal from some perspectives, but he is not the norm in America's high schools. Except for students in Advanced Placement courses, or in the elite independent schools we studied, students like Ryan are a distinct minority. Even many so-called mainstream students from middle-class, "white" backgrounds challenge their teachers' expectations. Teachers remark that they are often frustrated by students who fail to complete homework assignments, turn in sloppy work, are tired from after-school jobs, or grow restless and inattentive in class.[2] "They don't read!" exclaimed a disheartened teacher. Or they do not subscribe to the conventional goals that their school sets out for them. "Kids today just don't value education," complained a Michigan teacher. "They get so many things now, things are just given to them now. So why worry about getting an education? It's sad."

The majority of public school teachers in our sample reported in a survey that students in their classes were less prepared than students they had taught in previous years (65 percent), that the attitudes and habits students brought to class greatly reduced their chances for academic success (73 percent), and that students in their classes had more serious social and family problems than students they had taught in previous years (85 percent).

When discussing today's students, teachers often mention the challenges associated with changed family circumstances first, whether the students are long-term neighborhood residents or recent arrivals by court order, family move, or immigration. A Michigan teacher told us, "We have a lot of kids [who] have very little support at home, a lot of single parents . . . a lot of kids who don't even live at home." Teachers appreciate that parents

who are besieged by a plethora of contemporary pressures—
unstable domestic situations, lack of support for child rearing,
inadequate income, bleak job prospects, joblessness, homeless-
ness—have little time or energy, or sometimes even inclination,
to get involved in their children's school life. These changed
family realities cause many teachers to take a close look at their
own assumptions. "You have got to be sensitive to changes in
society, and how they're affecting kids," advised a California
teacher. "You can't say, 'Well, tell your parents' anymore because when you say 'parents' you've closed down 75 percent of
these kids."

Changed family circumstances also redefine traditional home-
school relations, many teachers remarked. A California biology
teacher bemoaning her inability to make contact with parents—
unreturned phone calls, ignored notes, missed conferences—
told us that she feels alone in her attempts to work with many
students. "A lot of times I contact the home and the home is
completely apathetic or unable, dysfunctionally unable, to help."

Teachers in one urban school used the expression "revolving
classroom doors" to capture their school's experience of student
transience and absenteeism, which mirror migration trends and
changed family circumstances. A Michigan teacher commented
that three different students had occupied some of the seats in
his classroom over a two-week period. "I think I counted close
to a thousand absences the first marking period. . . . I have got
kids right now I haven't seen for two weeks." This high rate of
student absence makes classroom routines, such as testing, difficult to manage: "I'm still waiting three weeks after I've given a
test for some people to show to take it." A California social studies teacher expressed frustration over never being able to "catch
up with all of them. You just pass out a book and get this kid
started, and two days later this one is gone and another comes
in and says, 'Where are we?'" An English teacher frustrated
with failed lesson plans and incomplete work confided, "no one
yet has figured out how do [a writing project for publication]
with kids who are here for a day or two and then gone for a day
or two . . . It is difficult in all literature classes to teach kids
who are just not here." In teachers' views, this level of classroom
"churn" has greater negative consequences for their practice
than do student mobility rates.

Public school teachers also comment on their students' juggling of school and personal demands. They mention an increasing number of teen pregnancies and the students they have lost as a result. A government teacher complained that "it is hard to stand up and talk about the Soviet Union when you have five young ladies [in your class] who are concerned about who is babysitting. It is difficult to get through about social concerns because they have so many themselves." Many lower-income students, especially girls, are unable to spend time on schoolwork because of heavy family responsibilities. Jobs compete, too. A math teacher told us: "There seems to be a general decline every year in the level at which students are functioning. [But what do you expect] when you have students walking in [who] are just totally exhausted because they're working all weekend, or they have worked the night before until ten or eleven at night . . . students that are putting in thirty hours a week just on their [outside] work."

Finally, teachers emphasize the social and cultural diversity of contemporary students as a factor that complicates their job. In the California districts we studied, high levels of immigration have brought students from an enormous variety of cultures and educational backgrounds to the public schools. Court-ordered desegregation has reassigned students to new schools. In many parts of the country, and in our sample of high schools, these changes in students' backgrounds have been rapid, abrupt, and found many teachers unprepared to respond.

Many California public school teachers we talked with, for example, felt overwhelmed by the cultures and languages of the students filling classroom seats formerly occupied by middle-class Anglo students. One teacher estimated that in her district, where one out of four students were classified as "limited English proficient" (LEP) or "non-English proficient" (NEP) in 1990; at least half of the students enrolled in the district's schools would be English learners in 2000. "The change has been phenomenal," a California mathematics teacher said. "Five years ago, we were not under court order. Five years ago, we were 6 to 8 percent minority; today we are about 56 percent nonwhite [and many students have little or no English]. It used to be that you'd teach advanced mathematics courses because nearly everybody was going to college. Now it is much more basic."

A science teacher remarked that she has only two classes in which "all the students can read and write in English." "In my two regular biology classes, nobody speaks English. There are about ten different languages in those classes," she said. A biology teacher in another California school echoed these frustrations as he described his efforts to teach science without materials comprehensible to his students: "What do you do with them when they don't know English? This [biology] text is written at a seventh-grade level. These students do not understand this text—they cannot understand it. Their reading level and their vocabulary, well . . ." But the issue is more complicated than his complaint suggests. In a tenth-grade social studies class, two young Spanish-speaking immigrants who entered the class at midyear—one from a rural region of Mexico and the other from Mexico City—were reading at widely different levels in their native language, the former at a fifth-grade level and the latter at an eleventh-grade level.

Furthermore, the majority of students migrating into American urban schools face the hurdle of poverty as well as language. "Five years ago," said a California high school principal, "we wanted to give a needy family a Christmas basket, and we couldn't find a needy family. This year we are feeding hundreds of kids breakfast and lunch every day."

Social-demographic trends continuing into the twenty-first century have brought students into high school classrooms who do not conform in appearance, comportment, or academic preparation to earlier generations of students, particularly as they are remembered by veteran teachers. They threaten teaching routines that assume students' academic readiness and reticence. Peggy Sue Thompson, a white teenager from a poor working-class family, is typical of many high school students today: she is indifferent to classroom schedules and assignments and largely disengaged from teachers' expectations. For many teachers, Peggy Sue's poor classroom performance raises tough questions about their practice. Should they attempt to cover conventional "scope and sequence"? Or should they respond in some different way to the challenges today's students pose for classroom practice? If so, what should be included or modified? The many-stranded, underlying question is, *How* might teachers better respond to students who bring to class challenges of diverse cultures, languages, levels of academic preparation—often without the family supports assumed by traditional school practice?

PATTERNS OF PRACTICE

Schoolteaching brings teachers and students together to address content. The classroom triangle of teacher, content, and student forms the core of professional practice and the essence of the schooling enterprise—the "stuff" of teaching.[3]

THE CLASSROOM TRIANGLE

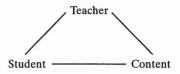

High school teachers' questions about how and what to teach today's students raise issues about the connections this triangle posits. How teachers go about the job of engaging students with content in their classroom reveals further questions about how they relate to students and how they construe their subject matter.

Constructions of Classroom Practice

We found that teachers' responses to questions of what and how to teach contemporary high school students varied in ways that had significant consequences for what happened in the classroom and what students learned. Some teachers expressed frustration and cynicism about their high school students; others spoke enthusiastically about what they and their students had accomplished. Some students slouched in their chairs and tuned out; others described their work in excited terms and pointed with pride to what they had done. Across classrooms, we saw teachers' interactions and relationships with their students range from distant and removed to personal and mutually engaged. For some teachers, the dynamics of the classroom expressed how they understood contemporary students—as merely different from those of just a few years ago, or as somehow lacking when measured against nostalgic conceptions of the "ideal." Similarly,

Table 2.1 Patterns of Teaching Practice in Contemporary Classrooms

Patterns of Practice	Dimensions of Classroom Practice			Education Outcomes
	Students	Content	Pedagogy	
Enact traditions of practice	Passive learner role	Subject static; knowledge given	Routine, teacher-centered	Success with traditional students only
Lower expectations and standards	Passive learner role	Watered-down subject matter	Routine, teacher-centered	Limited success with all students
Innovate to engage learners	Active learner role	Subject dynamic; knowledge constructed	Nonroutine, student-centered	Increased success with nontraditional students

teachers conveyed different kinds of relationships with the subject matter they taught. Some seemed merely to act as the transmitters of knowledge organized by curriculum developers and texts; others took an active role as learners in a dynamic field and crafters of curricula for particular students.

The classrooms we visited across the sixteen schools in our study generally followed three broad patterns of practice, depicted in table 2.1: enacting traditions, lowering expectations, and innovating to engage learners.[4] The dissimilar patterns of practice we saw signal teachers' different logics of practice, conceptions of their work and their students, and different consequences for both teachers and their students.

Enacting Traditions

Most commonly, teachers in the high schools we studied have responded to nontraditional students by maintaining conventional routines. They continue to teach as they have always taught, changing little in how they relate to their students or organize their subject instruction. Classroom practices remain largely teacher-centered, with lectures predominating. Subject content is taken as more or less given, and questions about how to teach Peggy Sue are answered in terms of "the guidelines." This pattern of practice follows a logic rooted in a professional culture that casts teacher as expert and student as recipient of knowledge. A California social studies teacher put it this way:

"Many teachers feel responsibility for transmitting information. They see this block of information and feel that for kids to be successful in life, they have to have everything planted in their brain. Almost as if you open the top of the head up, pour all of the information in, and seal it back up. To them, that would be the ideal way to teach. Doesn't matter who the students are." Teachers who operate from this logic tend to see students primarily in terms of deficiencies in their performance on standardized tests and define relationships with them accordingly.

A traditional Michigan English teacher, for example, described her students almost exclusively in terms of what they could *not* do with the material she presented:

> After I have gone over the story in the literature book . . . very slowly . . . I give them work so I can gather information about the kinds of things they're deficient in. Then I will select an area that the majority of the class is deficient in. But if there are a few people who are really not deficient in that area at all—and believe me that has happened—then I will give them a traditional writing assignment while I give the other people work on their deficiencies.

This mode of practice frames teacher-student relationships in relatively narrow and impersonal terms, and the teacher's role is seen primarily as filling in gaps in knowledge and skills.

In this respect, the high school teachers in our study resemble high school teachers around the country. Education historians describe the deep and robust roots of traditional teacher roles and classroom conventions: How teachers taught a hundred, fifty, or fifteen years ago is still how teachers teach today (Cuban 1984; Tyack and Tobin 1994). Traditional teaching practice follows established orthodoxy about what to cover and how to cover it—time-honored concepts of "scope and sequence." For example, most teachers in the schools we studied reported in a survey that their subject matter must be learned in a particular sequence (64 percent) and that covering all curriculum topics is very important (75 percent). Most teachers conduct their classroom instruction according to daily routines: 77 percent reported that their work tasks are the same from day to day; 76 percent rely on established procedures and practices.

Teachers who maintain traditional methods in response to the Peggy Sues in their classrooms generally express a high degree of certainty about their instructional decisions, a professional conviction rooted in time-honored disciplinary routines and conventional instructional roles.[5] For example, a Michigan mathematics teacher said: "I think my approach . . . is what you'd call a typical math presentation. We correct yesterday's assignment, we present new material, and then tomorrow we will do the sequence over." He raises few questions about his approach even though he also complains of students' inattention and poor performance.

Dan Lortie (1975) characterized this reliance on familiar routines as "reflexive conservatism." These classroom responses reflect a great deal about how teachers understand Peggy Sue's tardy work and indifference. Teachers keeping to traditions in the face of disappointing student performance tend to locate the problem in the student and to leave subject-area orthodoxy unexamined. A California English teacher, for example, despairs over the achievements of his tenth-grade students, whom he sees as "less prepared" and motivated than students he taught earlier in his career. His explanation focuses on students' lack of interest in the course content, which he assumes is fixed and immutable: "I happen to believe there should be a common body of knowledge. . . . Never before have I had so many students earning D's and F's in my classes."[6] A Michigan math teacher expresses a similar view when he describes the inadequate academic preparation of many students in his algebra classes. "Well, they have got to [have learned the basic material] a long time ago. There's not much I can really do about it. Either you fall in line [with my expectations], or you get out."

Teachers who frame the problem of disappointing student performance and indifference primarily in terms of student attributes generally understand their classroom task in terms of managing content. As an Esperanza English teacher put it, "I feel like my job is to do the best I can to teach that curriculum, whatever it happens to be. [But] I see so much apathy [among the students] that . . . I wouldn't place any bets on my success." Such teachers often justify their choices in terms of professional standards and the integrity of their subject domain: "I've got my standards." Some variation of this disheartened refrain emerged in almost every instance where we found teachers struggling to square poor student performance with past, often successful, teaching practices. Another example, this time from a math teacher at Valley High School railing against his students who failed to perform "up to standards":

> Oh man, you just sit here and you think how can anybody be that stupid . . . how can they be this damn stupid. The kid is where the problem is today. There is nothing wrong with the curriculum. If I could just get people that wanted to learn, then I could teach and everything would be wonderful.

Improved classroom outcomes, many traditional teachers believe, can come only from changed student attitudes and behavior.

For many teachers, maintaining traditions of teaching practice is a way to manage the tensions and uncertainties they face each day. However, when they interpret the problems represented by Peggy Sue and her peers largely as a lack of "good" students, they leave unexamined conventional beliefs about learning. Teachers who enact traditions in this more or less reflexive way effectively take relationships within the classroom triangle as a given, prescribed by time-honored norms. Though often frustrated and disappointed by what happens in their classrooms, they refuse to abandon the core principles of the profession, which hold teachers responsible for sustaining the integrity of the discipline as formalized curriculum and certifying students' mastery of course content and subject area skills.

Lowering Expectations and Standards

Other teachers respond to the tensions between their traditional conceptions of subject matter and teaching and their nontraditional students' attitudes, behaviors, and backgrounds by modifying their standards. Some adapt content to nontraditional students by covering less of the curriculum that typically is included in a conventional class and focus instead on remedying skill deficiencies; others cover standard topics but dilute the curricular content. A Rancho High School English teacher, for example, dropped most of the literature from his eleventh-grade English course so he could drill students in the grammar and reading skills he believed they needed before going on to consider literature. A biology teacher at Valley High School simply gave her limited-English-speaking students more time and repetition with worksheets. An Esperanza English teacher reduced his literature course to the bare bones for his nontraditional students, aiming for a "Cliff Notes sort of thing. I don't talk to them about the beauty of the language; I would be wasting my breath." In some instances, these curricular adaptations represent teachers' efforts to construct a supportive classroom environment for their students. In other cases, adaptation signals "dumbing down" and professional disinvestment.

Teachers who water down content for nontraditional students also locate the problem of disappointing classroom performance squarely on the students. For example, a teacher in Michigan confessed that he just does not put much effort into his teaching anymore since "the kids really don't care about getting an education anyway." His detached classroom presence and rote classroom practice communicate clearly his belief that "students today just aren't as good as the ones we used to have." In classes like this teacher's, traditional frames for classroom interactions are not replaced; they are modified, simplified, scaled-down, reduced. Subject performance norms change, but classroom roles generally do not.

A Michigan teacher provided this account of how she has managed her classroom of what she refers to as "lesser" students:

> *Interviewer:* What is on your mind when you begin your class?
> *Teacher:* I think the biggest thing on my mind is how to get them to be quiet. So now I have it pretty well regimented . . . they come in, sit down, I give them a short spiel, a tape, something. Then they go to work . . . their assigned tasks. These classes are pretty well on a bell curve, but on the down side of a bell curve. I just can't move very fast with those people. You can do many more things with the high-level youngster—it's more of a challenge, they are more eager and want a more diverse kind of lesson plan. Low-level you have to deal with so many things that aren't related to content.

Underlying this pattern of practice is teachers' belief that students who differ in one or another way from the "ideal" represented by Ryan Moore cannot engage "real" academic content. The ways in which the California and Michigan teachers have lowered their standards and expectations for these students reflect three subpatterns that Reba Page (1991) documented in ethnographic studies of lower-track classrooms in two high schools. In each, grade-level course content is revised or supplanted: in the "skeleton" pattern, a superficial version of the curriculum is covered at a slower pace; in the "skills" pattern, students are drilled on basic skills and facts that they lack; and in the "relevance" pattern, new content is invented to be fun and personally meaningful. Each pattern, in turn, builds upon a particular view of subject knowledge—as a system of concepts to be understood (more deeply by some), as a hierarchy of basic skills and higher-level knowledge, as relative to life circumstances and futures (Page 1991, 179–207).

In our observations, as in the classrooms that Page studied, most teachers who lower standards and expectations for students embrace all three approaches to revising their course content. For example, a typical class period in Mr. Morrison's tenth-grade biology class in Oak Valley High School includes a ten-minute lecture on a concept such as tensile strength, ten to twenty minutes of quiet time on a worksheet that requires students to copy definitions of several science terms from their textbook, and twenty to thirty minutes for students to "feel comfortable" in class by playing with a pet white rat or talking with friends.

This general pattern of lowering standards is most prevalent in low-track classes in the comprehensive schools we studied. However, it is also common in regular classes taught by teachers who perceive a decline in their students' academic preparation for the course. Teachers sometimes feel torn between loyalty to the curriculum and its content standards and the need to support students and avoid high failure rates. In either case, the result is that students are less engaged in what they are learning and demonstrate less mastery of subject content. However, the third pattern of teaching practice we observed offers a vision of innovation that avoids this dilemma by reconstituting all the elements of the classroom triangle.

Innovating to Engage Students in High-level Content

Some teachers respond to strains between traditional norms of classroom practice and students who depart from them by re-thinking assumptions about subject matter, students, and how to connect them. These teachers move beyond or outside estab-lished frames for instruction to find or develop content and class-room strategies that will enable students to master core subject concepts. We saw high school teachers making changes of the most fundamental sort along all "legs" of the classroom trian-gle—relations between students and content, between teacher and content, and between teacher and student.

Student-content relations. In this pattern of practice, teachers work to establish an active role for students in developing new, deeper subject knowledge that builds upon their interests, skills, and prior knowledge. These teachers, knowingly or not, move toward "teaching for understanding"—emphasizing depth in students' content knowledge over coverage of many topics and skills, and problem-solving skills over mastery of the kinds of routines emphasized in conventional instruction (for elabo-ration, see Cohen, McLaughlin, and Talbert 1993; Bransford, Brown, and Cocking 1999).

Instructional materials are among the first elements of prac-tice to be rethought when high school teachers seek new ways to involve students in content. California teachers particularly wrestle with problems of how to provide challenging work for students whose English-language skills or formal academic back-ground has ill-prepared them for high school. An Esperanza mathematics teacher told us that rethinking practice requires ob-serving how students engage subject matter. Rather than follow-ing the prescribed mathematics text, for example, this teacher moved to an experience-based approach to promote students' understanding of math fundamentals. She got rid of her text-books and worked with manipulatives instead as a way to con-nect her students to mathematics. "The tangible is the language of all people."

Taking her students' perspective, she has found they learn more successfully and are more comfortable with this approach to math instruction. "There is no text book [in my basic math course]," she told us. "Those kids don't want to carry books around anyway. They don't like the way it looks to be seen with a book—people make fun of them." She builds her class upon her observation that her students are "very tactile and visually oriented."

> I just have a philosophy that I am looking for [a] totally *different,* off-the-wall way to introduce a topic, follow up on it, and relate to a kid's world. They respond very well to hands-on stuff. This group of kids has just *finished* work[ing] with multiplying binomials and factoring trinomial—algebra skills—using manipulatives, little rectangles and squares. They can see how to represent $x^2 + 5x + 6$ and then see how to rearrange [the manipulatives] so they can actually factor it. Today I took a group of [limited English proficient] kids who never had any algebra through reciprocals, through squares, square roots, cubes, cube roots, and they understand what they're doing, and they're having a good time.

She counts this approach a success, "more than even I thought it would be. Right now I have about a third to a half of these kids who will go on to an algebra class, and usually its only two or three." Her quest for innovative classroom practices reflects her view that contemporary students are different from yesterday's and need different classroom strategies for them to succeed: "I think of them as kids who are turned off to math rather than kids who are too stupid to learn. It's a different philosophy and the kids like it. They still may not like math, but it's better than anything else they've had before."

Other teachers working to develop effective strategies for engaging their nontraditional students in learning higher-order subject concepts also emphasize the visual and hands-on practices they find to be more successful than traditional methods. Ironically, one of these strategies involves new uses for that old classroom technology the chalkboard. Math teachers in Esperanza highlight the value of students' work at the board in terms of making visible the development of a proof or solution to a problem. Board work, said one, "lets you give constant feedback. Lets you see those thought processes. One of my most effective ways of communicating with kids who have language problems is [to] have them do board problems. I can see in an instant if they're understanding it, communicating it, and make adjustments immediately." An Oak Valley science teacher whose classroom buzzes with students' engagement with basic physics counts the chalkboard as critical to his success: "I use it to map concepts visually—to show them how concepts relate, like distance and time. I write things down I want them to have in their notes, like when they have done their own graphs, it goes up on the board. But the thing is how I spatially arrange it so the visual becomes a kind of summary of their work." Other teachers use overhead projectors for the same purpose and as a medium for students to show their peers how they have approached a complex problem.

Various forms of group work also express new ways of connecting students to content in innovative high school classrooms. A social studies teacher devised his own version of cooperative learning, putting students into five groups where "they read, debate, negotiate, and decide what's most important in an essay or chapter. Then each group makes a summary and gives it to the class. We have a quiz based on these sheets, and they love it because its all student generated. Then they do a presentation, and these are unbelievable. I mean, they've spent time after school, they go to people's houses to work on them, it's gone way beyond. And now some of the kids want to do presentations for the eighth-grade U.S. history class. This is so great—these are kids who are really at the margins and barely there in other classes." We saw similar strategies in other classrooms where nontraditional kids were enthusiastically learning. An English teacher uses writing groups; a math teacher creates groups of three ("no more than that," he advises); a science teacher has all but abandoned texts and instead connects students through lab-based group projects. Teachers explain the value of this strategy in terms of peer assistance and the added sense of autonomy students feel. "They are able to work in their own style, and strike their own path. It really makes a difference in the quality of the work they produce," said an English teacher. A California math teacher believes that groups also provide an important sense of security for her students: "All of my classes are in little clusters, groups of four. I can lecture when I want, make group assignments, explorations. They function very well as a group. There's no more fear of the teacher—It's like they have help, so they say 'if I can't do it maybe one of my *compadres* can.' So I am no longer the fear factor I would be in a 'sit down, shut up, take notes' situation where the only thing they are allowed to do is take notes."

All teachers who struggle to engage students underscore the importance of finding ways to make content germane. A California math teacher explained: "We have to have relevance, something that relates to their lives. Something they can use and fall back on when they haven't had a formula pounded into their heads." An English teacher advised: "In order for them to fully understand or appreciate the literature, I think they need to see it as a reflection of life. By relating what we read to their lives I can help them make that connection. Like when we began *To Kill a Mockingbird,* I asked them to remember their childhood and was there anyone on their block they were afraid of."

Teacher-content relations. Intimately tied up with teachers' innovations to engage nontraditional students is their own relationship with the discipline. Teachers' conceptions and understandings of their subject matter evolve and deepen as they find new ways of working with their students. Across high schools and subjects, teachers whose practice can be described as "innovative" have ideas about what students most need to learn that depart in significant ways from what conventional curricula dictate. In one or another way, these teachers emphasize students' understanding of "patterns" and "concepts," the importance of "thinking about problems." The views of an Oak Valley science teacher about how he has succeeded in challenging and engaging his classes of diverse learners sound a lot like those we heard in other innovative classrooms: "What I am trying to do is to teach the kids to think. I am trying to get them to understand something, not just the topic I am teaching Tuesday at two. But what are the underlying principles? What are commonalities? So no matter what I try to teach, that same approach works."

For innovative teachers, "that same approach" means involving students quickly in concepts and problem solving, and working with basic skills separately. "You have to tap into their intellect," says the Oak Valley science teacher. "You'll kill their interest if you use content to teach basic skills. I teach the skill area independent of content. I hammer on the skills, I mean they do it every day, all the time. But they do it as homework. Graphing skills for example. I make up a bunch of crazy data like compare the profits of Metallica versus Billy Idol. So you start to graph. And they graph it. [Without that practice,] if I had tried this lab today [which assumed graphing skills], it would have been totally impossible. But it wasn't impossible today. And I get a 90 percent return rate on homework. I can get the homework in because I am giving them homework in the skill area that they can now see applied to content."

Crafting new classroom content and creating opportunities for students to go deeply into a subject constitute primary challenges for teachers attempting to innovate in their instruction. Many teachers' own knowledge of a subject is relatively shallow, and they struggle to achieve a deeper understanding of concepts and their linkages in order to guide their students' learning more effectively. Furthermore, the professional resources available for teacher learning and for curricular innovations vary widely from school to school and from department to department. As we describe in chapters 3 and 4, a collaborative community of practice in which teachers share instructional resources and reflections on practice appears essential to their persistence and success in innovating classroom practice.

Teacher-student relations. Innovative patterns of practice also depart from traditional teacher-dominated instructional roles to establish student-centered classroom environments in which teachers facilitate student work and learning. Teachers describe their efforts to "really listen" to their students and understand the classroom from their perspective. For example, a Dover High School math teacher's experience as a student government sponsor forced her to rethink long-held assumptions about practice:

> One of the things I found [is] that I had to go back and rewrite a lot of the ways I teach kids because of the fact that society has changed the way it raises kids . . . no textbook fits that group of thirty kids you have in the classroom. It used to be that as long as I knew enough math, I could teach any kid. But now I've got some empathy for what that kid has gone through . . . now they are not trained to listen to their teacher, so I've got to retrain myself to listen to them.

Another teacher put it this way: "I can't be hiding behind the textbook, the shut-up sheets, or the test every Friday, lecture and cranking on through, if I want to really see what's going on."

One manifestation of this move to more personal relations in the classroom is the sort of feedback teachers give students. Teachers stress the importance of noticing "small wins":

> Constantly reminding them they are really good, very success-
> ful, you know, rising to the occasion . . . and they start to be-
> lieve they can be successful. Why do [I] give partial credit?
> To encourage them . . . to say, hey you got this started right,
> you did something right, I'll give you credit for that. Let's
> see if we can't build on that and get it right. It's easy to go
> through and just mark them all wrong.

Some of the most difficult changes that veteran teachers need to make in their relations with students involve conventional ideas about classroom management. A California social studies teacher said: "You know it's an evolution—really an evolution, letting control go . . . you know, wanting the kids to sit in their seats with their feet on the floor, hands on the desk, kind of mentality." Across the board, we heard that this "evolution" entails changing strategies for dealing with classroom disruptions and behavioral problems. Almost all of the teachers we interviewed commented that they did not "make referrals," that is, send students to the principal's office for discipline, but prefer to work out behavioral problems themselves. One teacher said he requires students to attend his seventh-period class, where they can do their homework. Another calls classroom timeouts. One uses journals as a way for students to express problems they are having in the classroom and to open up communication. "Sending a kid to the office," said a math teacher, "just doesn't fit the kind of environment I am trying to create in my class-room."

A California teacher who sees today's students as generally unlike but no less able than yesterday's, told us how, in his view, teachers need to be aware of aspects of students' lives tradition-ally considered outside their professional purview:

> Some teachers still see it as yes/no, wet/dry, black/white. It
> can't be that anymore. Back in the fifties, if I had Beaver and

Wally and those guys in class, sure, because the role of the teacher back then was a lot more clearly defined. The role of the teacher now is pretty broad. We're not there just to instruct or to transmit information. We've got to be parents in some cases, we've got to be counselors, we've got to be disciplinarians, we've got to be cops, we've got to be a lot of different things. If you're not flexible, you're going to burn out real good. The situation's always changing, every day is different. But the kids are great, and this makes it exciting. They make it fun. Teachers who think of teaching and learning this way tend to see students primarily in terms of their performance and define relationships with them accordingly.

Teachers who reject a logic of practice that conveys "blocks of knowledge" to students typically make efforts to know students as individuals with particular strengths, experiences, knowledge, and areas for development. An English teacher whose classes reflect the warm, easy relationships she has with her students, told us "every class I plan is different. Even if I am presenting the same information, my approach will vary according to the needs of my students. It usually takes me two or three weeks at the beginning of the year to become accustomed to their diverse personalities and different learning styles." Both her practice and her relations with students build upon this diversity and a logic of practice that is, in her words, "student-centered and active. Forget didactic instruction! [My students] want to participate, they really want to be there, to share in the instruction and to share in the learning."

These teachers believe that the poor fit between contemporary students and traditional instruction is the source of problems in many high school classrooms—not student "deficiencies" as assessed against nostalgic ideals. Innovating teachers also interpret changes in their students as permanent ones, as signs of changed American society, not as an irritating exception to conventional standards of a "good student" or "real school." Esperanza's vice principal charged her faculty to reconsider practice in these terms: "The demographics . . . it's *happening,* you can't *stop it* . . . if you don't like it, you'd better look for another job . . . [I told the faculty that] we have choices: we can either keep this school a top academic school, or we can wallow around in 'poor me.' And so over the years, I think the teachers have kept their expectations high [as they rethought practice for their students]."

An Ibsen social studies teacher, whose lively class engaged traditional and nontraditional students alike, told us: "Those who continue to teach in a traditional way . . . they're running head on into a student who is not like the student they taught back in the sixties or seventies or even the eighties. It's a different generation of Americans now, so we have to deal with them [in different ways]." Using the example of a former gang member, an African-American student doing B work in his college preparatory history course, this teacher underscored the importance of changing practices to match students' learning styles: "In a traditional classroom, I don't think he'd be very successful, because different things motivate him. I look at his report card, and I see that teachers who have my style, he does well in. Other teachers who say, 'Answer the questions, do the worksheet, da, da, da,' he doesn't do well in their classes." In this teacher's classroom, ideas form the starting point for discourse, rather than a final product reified in worksheets and multiple-choice tests.

HOW TEACHING PATTERNS AFFECT STUDENTS

Teachers' different responses to contemporary students—the patterns of practice they pursue in their classrooms, and the conceptions of students and principles of teaching from which they derive—fundamentally shape students' classroom experiences.[7]

Students like Ryan Moore, cited by his teachers as an "ideal student," often find comfort in traditional high school routines and the teachers who enact them. Ryan appreciates knowing what to expect and how to get good grades. He explained why he chose a particular class as his favorite in just these terms: "There's nothing left to question . . . our assignments are there, and it's clear so we know what we have to do." Ryan's formula for success in high school reflects the norms and relationships of classrooms found in American classrooms since the turn of the century: "Basically you just do your work and you listen and you take notes and everything . . . Yeah, it's basically—it's all the same" (Phelan, Davidson, and Yu 1998, 38–39). Even while he values the control these established routines provide, Ryan also knows some of the costs of conforming to teachers' expectations. He told us that he likes writing, and that it is "fun until you have to do it for a grade. . . . It's fun to write but I always worry that I'm going to get a bad grade [if I write the way I'd like to] when I do it for school. So it seems like for school you have to write the way your teacher wants you to write."[8]

However, other students, such as Peggy Sue Thompson, often struggle in these teacher-directed, sometimes impersonal classrooms. Even academically successful nontraditional students find such classrooms difficult. For example, a high-achieving Latina at Valley described her experience with the math teacher who feels all of his students are "the problem":

> Ooh . . . I dread that class . . . I didn't do well. At the end I got a B, but it wasn't what I was hoping for . . . it was a hard class, because he didn't really explain the material. It was like he taught college also at the same time that he teaches high school. So it's sort of like, he brought those techniques to high school. And he'd move around really quick, and you couldn't follow him. And it was just really difficult.

However, most of her peers, who ride with her on the bus from across town, cannot manage in this setting and fail in large numbers. In our sample of schools, we saw that nontraditional students generally fare poorly in traditional classrooms, reinforcing teachers' negative attitudes about "today's students."

A steady diet of frustration is a major source of professional exhaustion for teachers. One Michigan social studies teacher equated lack of teacher adaptation with just such "burnout."

> Because of [a student's] environment, because he comes into school less equipped than other kids, am I going to call him a failure? No way. However, I see a lot of teachers who won't buy into that [view of the student and maintain conventional practices]. That's what burns teachers out, you know. They come and in try to lecture for fifty-five minutes to kids whose attention span might be ten . . . and then they fail them rather than think about ways they could do things differently in their classroom.

Although she herself used to be a very traditional teacher, she has changed her view: "Whenever I wake up and find myself doing the same thing I did five years ago, then I think it's time to move on to something else, because I think I'm no longer doing the kids any good . . . you've gotta be real sensitive to changes in society and how they're affecting kids."

Teachers who understand their nontraditional students in these terms speak with one voice in saying that changes in classroom practices are essential not only to meet the needs of contemporary students, but also to support teachers' sense of efficacy:

> Teachers have been used to lecturing and leading the lesson . . . and they aren't getting satisfaction from kids' achievement now, because they aren't achieving. We need to grow and change and evolve too. We were talking this morning about the different ideas of teacher as worker and teacher as dispenser of information. [Teachers who adhere to] the latter are finding it difficult to perform now since the students are not the same.

Alternatively, when traditional teachers reduce their expectations and standards to accommodate students' perceived shortcomings, both teachers and students disengage from subject matter. Many students tune out in classrooms where less is asked of them and less is provided to them. An Onyx Ridge English teacher relayed a passionate plea from a student seeking entry to her college preparatory class: "A kid told me yesterday, 'I want to be here, I would rather learn something and fail this class than be in a [lower-level] class again. I'm sorry but I'll drop out if I am in a [lower-level] class again.'" Teachers also tune out when operating in unchallenging instructional settings.

Sonia Navarro, a Latina attending the same school as Ryan Moore, described her English class as characterized by "seatwork"—in this case, short question-and-answer sessions led by the teacher. "You can't talk in there because if you talk you go to in-house suspension. . . . It's strict and there's hardly ever group work . . . so nobody's talking, we just read, read, read— and that's all we do." She contrasted her boredom and failure in such classes with her engagement in classes where teachers make an effort to get to know her and involve students more actively.

Students also are keenly aware of how their teachers see them. Just as traditional students like Ryan Moore understand that they are perceived as "good" students and manage to elicit continued approval from their teachers, sometimes nontraditional students experience school and their teachers' responses to them as negative. Students of color, in particular, resent what they perceive as disrespect or low expectations from their teachers, even when they do well in school. A Latina who rides the bus from her low-income, racially mixed neighborhood and who maintains a 3.85 GPA at Valley High School, feels that "nobody notices you . . . because they don't want to be expecting too much. . . . They don't give you credit for who you are. You're just there, because like really if an older person sees you walking down the street, they go 'oh, another low-life'" (Phelan, Davidson, and Yu 1998, 75–76).

Students who are not succeeding, or who are just going through the motions in their lower-track courses, rightly or wrongly interpret teachers' low expectations in terms of racial stereotypes. A Filipina-American student at Rancho told us that her teacher was "kind of racist in a way . . . just the way she talks, you know. If she's talking about a bad neighborhood, she'll say the black kids. The whites are all in the good neighborhoods and stuff . . . And then just stuff, she'll just, whenever we talk about bad people, she'll mention blacks and gangs. All the black people are bad" (Davidson 1996, 41). In the same vein, Sonia, whose dress and makeup express her loyalty to Latina culture in her racially divided high school, discussed how she thinks her teachers view her:

> *Sonia:* It's like once they see a Mexican—right away, you know, especially when they are dressed like this, you know . . . I wear a lot of eyeliner or something, you know, we look scary-looking sometimes, you know? I guess that's the way teachers are. . . . Most teachers—you know, white teachers— some of them are kind of prejudiced.
>
> *Interviewer:* What makes you know that?
>
> *Sonia:* It's probably the way they look at you, the way they talk, you know when they're talking about something

like when they talk about people who are going to drop out
. . . And when [a teacher talks] about teenage pregnancy or
something like that. He turns around and looks at us [the
Latinas in the class]. It's like, he tries to look around the
whole room so we won't notice but like he mostly tries to get
it through our heads, you know. Sometimes I think he's preju-
diced. (Davidson 1996, 129–30)

Sonia expressly resented the fact that many of her teachers
do not really know her. "They should always look at what a person has. They have to talk to that person, get to know that person" rather than drawing stereotypical conclusions about interests and ability. Sonia's anger over some of her teachers' efforts
to make the curriculum culturally relevant echoes experiences
of students in the classes Reba Page described. As Page put it:
"Ironically, these 'relevant' lessons anger students as much as
or more than they interest them. They confuse classroom participants' prerogatives and responsibilities and set in motion a cycle
in which teachers' control grows increasingly arbitrary and calls
forth student responses that are increasingly aggressively passive" (1991, 194). Ironically, teachers who try to construct "relevant" lessons by focusing on students' age, gender, ethnicity,
race, academic status, inferred interests, or futures often alienate
the students they aim to reach.

Nontraditional students appear to be more at home and successful as learners in classrooms where teachers connect them
to subjects in new ways. The students we interviewed recognized
and appreciated teachers' efforts to get to know them and to
create classroom settings that encouraged academic engagement
and expression of ideas. Yet nontraditional students describe
most of their classes as highly structured, teacher-controlled, and
regimented (For elaboration, see Phelan, Davidson, and Cao
1992).

Sonia's life sciences class is her favorite. Her teacher distinguishes himself from his colleagues in establishing personal,
rather than categorical, relationships with students: "I have always tried to find something about everyone. . . . It helps that
[students] know that there's something good about themselves,
because they may not hear it for years"(Phelan, Davidson, and
Cao 1992, 135). Sonia responds to this personalized classroom

environment with a high level of engagement and accomplishment, in stark contrast to her silent withdrawal in more traditional classes. She describes how her teacher gets students involved in what they're learning: "You ask him a question, and [un]like most teachers [he] doesn't just give you the answer . . . he makes you think about the question and then he gives you the clues, and then you have to figure it out yourself. . . . I like that, because he makes you think" (Phelan, Davidson, and Yu 1998, 136).

Snapshots of students' responses to classrooms representing an innovative pattern of instruction illustrate how their personal engagement translates into learning and a sense of accomplishment. Thomas, a student with limited language skills, tells us how "great" his social studies class is. "We really get a chance to talk about things and to figure stuff out for ourselves. He respects our opinions a lot. Even when my writing isn't real good, I can say what I think and what we found out in our group. I am doing good in that class because it is never boring." Students also stress the importance of the changed student roles and relationships they encountered in innovative classrooms. Robert talks about how his English teacher's strategy of cooperative learning groups benefited all members in both academic and social ways:

> She read the names and it was kind of the luck of the draw.
> You could end up in a group of people you despise . . . but
> at the end of the year people go to the front of the room and
> give a short speech on what the year meant to them, and I
> don't think I have ever seen more people cry in a group. The
> harmony—because working together and then even some people, even the stupidest idea wouldn't be overlooked. Everybody seemed to be like a valid contributor to the classroom.
> (Phelan, Davidson, and Yu 1998, 150–51)

We visited schools in which the kinds of students who would have been turned off and tuned out in most urban high schools instead talked to us animatedly about learning and about their schoolwork. In an alternative high school for youth who were not succeeding in a "regular" high school, for example, we listened to students' critiquing Hemingway, and then reading their own writing and commenting to peers on ways to strengthen theirs. In an urban school dedicated to the performing arts, we found students intent on their writing, music, and staging the school's dramatic production. In a school across town, students with the same social and economic background made C's, D's, or F's in their schoolwork—and dropped out in large numbers.

~~~

How is it that teachers make such fundamentally different responses to the challenge of engaging today's high school students in meaningful academic work? Why is teaching practice in these high schools much more varied than analysts of the teaching profession lead us to expect (for example, Cuban 1984; Tyack and Tobin 1994)? Our inquiry turned to focus on the contexts of the distinctive patterns of teaching practice we found. What differences in the circumstances of teachers' work makes one or another pattern more likely?

Clearly social class matters. We found traditional teaching patterns to be more prevalent in the college preparatory private schools we studied (Paloma and Juliet Wright), in the suburban California and Michigan high schools (Oak Valley and Dover), and in the urban school serving middle-class students (Onyx Ridge). In these settings where students are acclimated to traditional classrooms and are up to grade-level standards in subject curricula, veteran teachers' routines are not significantly challenged.

It was in the schools serving highly diverse student populations that we found the most divergent patterns of teaching practice. Many teachers in these settings lowered their expectations and standards for student learning. This pattern was especially common in the low-track classes of comprehensive high schools (Rancho and Valley in California, Washington Academy and LaSalle in Michigan). As we discuss in chapter 4, teachers assigned to low-track classes are often themselves poorly prepared in the subject and new to teaching.

However, we also found teachers in these schools who have successfully engaged their nontraditional students in challenging academics. They teach in schools and departments with a strong professional community committed to making innovations that support student and teacher learning and success. The next two chapters portray the professional communities that support particular patterns of teaching practice. We use strategic case comparisons—two subject departments in Adobe Viejo's Oak Valley High School, two math departments in demographically similar Mostaza district high schools, three mission schools serving nontraditional students—to illuminate qualitative differences in the high school teaching communities we found.

CHAPTER 3

Communities of Teaching Practice

Teaching practice reflects a teacher's ideas about each "leg" of the classroom triangle—conceptions of subject matter and knowledge, beliefs about students in the class, and notions of effective pedagogy. Most consequential for what happens in the classroom, however, appears to be a teacher's view of the students' abilities, motivation, interests, and engagement with school. Differences in the ways that teachers understand their nontraditional students—as deficient or as different—frame the divergent patterns of classroom practice sketched in chapter 2. Moreover, particular understandings of students develop and persist within the cultures of high school professional communities.

Consider, for example, views of the same kind of students held by math teachers in Valley High School and in Esperanza High School. Valley's bitter math teacher understands his classroom disappointments in terms of "the kid today": "The faculty feels, 'We had a perfectly good school and look what they have done to us [with new student assignment policies].' We're getting everyone's castoffs—we're just providing baby-sitting. We're grappling with a problem that has no solution." (The Valley vice principal suggested that this teacher's attitude about the students who come to Valley High School as part of the busing program is shared by many of his colleagues: "The teachers here are used to teaching white, middle-class students. It is really hard for a lot of them to adjust. An underlying attitude on the part of many teachers is that the minority kids are the problem.") This math teacher practices in a school with wide agreement across departments that students are deficient, and lowered expectations define the dominant pattern of classroom teaching.

In contrast, the Esperanza math teacher who successfully took her limited-English students through cube roots praised their energy and hard work. She said that "the mix of backgrounds and talents in this school is just exhilarating—at some schools I know it is merely tolerated, or just seen as something to endure. Here this student diversity enriches. I like these kids . . . they certainly are not complacent! They are much more creative and outgoing." Furthermore, she stressed, "we have expectations in math regardless of language limitations . . . we don't want to lower the standards to accommodate a lack of language." Her comments about expectations and standards—note her use of "we"—reflect the strong, innovative professional community of Esperanza's math department.

We found that highly divergent beliefs about today's students develop and persist in high school professional communities. In some schools we studied, whole faculties share an understanding of their nontraditional students and the problems for practice they pose. In other schools, teachers in different subject departments embrace divergent views of the same students. Although many schools and departments we studied are characterized by weak professional communities in which teachers keep their thoughts and practice private, a number stand out as strong teaching cultures that significantly shaped teachers' classroom practice. In these communities of practice, teachers are mutually engaged in teaching; they jointly develop their practice; and they share a repertoire of resources and history.[1] In some communities of practice we found, teachers' joint enterprise is defined by teaching orthodoxies and deficit views of nontraditional students; in others, a belief that all students can meet high academic standards defines the enterprise. For better or worse in terms of students' experiences and learning opportunities, professional communities are consequential contexts of high school teaching.

SCHOOL CHARTERS AND TEACHING PRACTICE

Strong school missions have forged communities of practice in a few of the schools we studied. In the private and alternative schools, teacher community builds around enacting the school's mission or "charter" to address their students' particular futures or pasts. In these schoolwide communities, teachers and students have a sense of mutual purpose, and a similar understanding of and expectations for their respective roles. Classroom environments are more or less of a piece with the school's special cultural fabric.

In Paloma and Juliet Wright, two independent college-preparatory schools, most students embody attributes of the traditional "good" high school student—that is, the student who is college-bound, eager to achieve in terms of class demands, and compliant with classroom routines. In these settings, teachers find little in their students to oppose traditional ideas of subject matter or role. And, except for some modern technical accouterments, these classrooms look and feel like the high school classrooms we attended years ago—and that continue to typify American high schools.

Teachers in these school communities construct their practice around concepts of the "good" class, the "good" student, and "good" educational futures. A Paloma teacher said: "The thing here isn't just going to college—that's not what's important. It's *what* college." The high-paced, demanding setting at this elite school epitomizes traditional classroom roles and practices. Teachers' work is defined almost entirely in terms of ensuring highest levels of student academic achievement and the professional satisfaction and prestige they derive from their students' success. "Knowledge" at Paloma is considered in time-honored institutional terms: subject-area canons and the admissions requirements of prestigious colleges and universities. Paloma teachers confront little uncertainty as they develop their classroom practices. While at least one teacher worries that there is too little regard for the student as "a total human being rather than as something to be educated," and many express concern that students work under too much pressure, the faculty culture revolves around academic excellence, as conventionally understood and prized.

Paloma teachers are proud when their graduates tell them that work at Harvard, Stanford, or Princeton "isn't as hard" as it is at Paloma. Paloma's performance standards are high indeed. The English curriculum, for example, offers only honors and Advanced Placement courses. Expectations escalate within some classrooms. An English teacher tells us, "There are always two or three in each class who are very able. I teach to the strongest. I set the standards by the three strongest. If I can reach two or three out of fifteen or eighteen, that's the most I can expect." This teacher's views about students struggling in her high-octane Shakespeare course make it clear that she is teaching a subject, not students: "Some of the foreign-born Asian students are barely making C's in my course. They have both conceptual and linguistic problems. The nuances, the fine points, and my pace are all difficult for them. [But] they elect to take on the risk when they choose my course." In the ultimate separation of student and subject matter, she recommended that the dean of studies "advise them not to take the Shakespeare course."

Juliet Wright likewise defines good teaching in terms of high-status knowledge and college admissions but sets classroom pace and demands a notch lower than Paloma's. Students at Juliet Wright work hard to achieve. "Love it or not, they'll perform," the Advanced Placement chemistry teacher told us. "These kids are really cooperative. They want the high grade point average that this weighted AP course will give them if they do well. I don't have one kid in here who is going to give me trouble or not go with the flow." The looser charter of this college-preparatory school defines a somewhat weaker school community than we found in Paloma.

In both college-preparatory schools, teachers are bound together by their school's charter and its norms of professional practice; in this respect they are part of a strong professional community. However, their classroom teaching tends to be both individual and highly organized by specialized subject traditions; and in this respect they are *not* strong communities of practice. These cases, as compared with their private and public school counterparts in our sample, highlight the key roles that student diversity and change play in both challenging traditions of high school teaching practice and engendering joint enterprise among teachers.

Two other secondary schools we studied also have strong school-level professional communities with goals, values, and practices that differ dramatically from those found at Paloma and Juliet Wright. Greenfield, a private California high school, and Prospect, an alternative public school in Michigan, have charters based on their very different student clientele and the schools' goals for them. Both schools work with students who have not "made it" in conventional high school settings. Teachers at these alternative high schools push subject-matter curriculum guides to the background as they focus on connecting their disaffected students to school and mainstream institutions, as well as to academic disciplines. The challenge of teaching at Greenfield and Prospect does not lie in fostering high scores on Advanced Placement tests, but in engaging students in academics while "getting them through."

Teachers in both schools carefully craft classroom activities and content with the objective of deepening students' engagement with their discipline and with the schooling enterprise. Greenfield's teachers generally view their students as academically talented but turned off. They hold students and themselves to relatively high standards of accomplishment, but rethink content to connect it with students' everyday interests. They go for depth in content, rather than the breadth of topical coverage prized in a traditional American high school curriculum. "Just pick three major concepts you want to get across and go with that," said Greenfield's English teacher. For example, the algebra teacher created problems that tapped students' interests in weight lifting and bodybuilding. The chemistry teacher developed an assay of popular adolescent products such as hair spray, soft drinks, toothpaste, and car wax to involve his students in the chemical analyses and understandings that are typically addressed using packaged chemicals, solutions, and laboratory manuals.

Prospect teachers depart even further from traditional practice in their efforts to engage students in academic work. Across subject domains, teachers endeavor to convey care, concern, and encouragement along with core discipline content. Prospect students' achievement level, as rated by teachers, falls at the bottom of our sample. Yet teachers see their students' poor academic performance primarily in terms of personal problems and lack of self-esteem, rather than deficiencies in learning abilities. "They're not 'bad' students, they just have a lot of bad stuff in their lives," said an English teacher. Teachers work through the medium of their subject area to reach students and help them to envision positive futures. Prospect's "course of study" consequently contains decidedly nontraditional entries: "Marriage and Divorce," "Drugs/Decisions," and "Home Repair." Teachers at both schools emphasize the importance of pace, as well as relevance. Prospect's principal said: "Our students can't sit in their classes. That's why some of [them] are here, really: attention spans. It's important to have a variety of activities." Teachers in Prospect work across subject areas to forge thematic topics to engage their students in active learning roles; they share and develop a broad repertoire of practices to support student learning in their classrooms.

In terms of teachers' stated intentions—of meeting student needs and keeping their attention—practice constructed in Greenfield and Prospect sounds like the pattern we described in chapter 2 as "lowering standards and expectations," or the "relevance mode" of teaching that Reba Page describes (1991, 190–96). However, these high school communities explicitly strive to connect students to the core concepts of their academic disciplines. Teachers' practice is rooted in shared respect for their nontraditional learners and in schoolwide structures and practices that support students' social and academic success. The strong professional community of these schools engenders innovative practices that avoid watered-down content and stereotypic notions of nontraditional students' needs and interests.

◆◆◆

Teachers working in these four special mission schools face little uncertainty in thinking about how to connect students and subject matter—how to construct the classroom triangle. Except at Prospect, where teachers are assigned by district policies, members of the faculty opt to teach in these school environments because they identify with the school mission and philosophy. "It's invisible," said a Paloma history teacher of the strong school culture, "but it's there. No one is here who doesn't want to be." Similarly, teachers who make their way to Greenfield expressly reject traditional roles and classroom routines for themselves and their students. A Greenfield English teacher said she "loves working with messed-up kids. It is my favorite thing to do because they aren't boring—they are interesting kids. I don't know what it would be like to be in a class . . . where everybody raises their hands and gives monotone answers . . . these kids never give teachers those pat answers." At neither Greenfield nor Prospect would Ryan Moore be the "ideal."

The homogeneous student body, small school size, and clear school focus and educational philosophy of these four special-purpose schools underpin high levels of agreement about desirable relationships between teachers and students and effective means to connect students to subject matter. Only in these mission schools did we see a school-level community of practice.

Indeed, conditions conducive to such communities exist in few public schools in our sample—or, from what we can see, in few American secondary schools in general. Most teachers in the large comprehensive high schools we studied wrestled with the challenges presented by their students' diverse cultures, languages, preparation, supports, and academic skills. Within and across these schools, we observed substantial differences in how teachers understand similar, or sometimes the same, students. We saw no school-level pattern in how teachers chose to connect students and content.

In typical large secondary schools, teachers' perceptions of students and the classroom contexts they construct for them vary widely. School does not comprise a community of practice for teachers. Rather, subject departments are the hands-on professional "home" for teachers, and departments can differ significantly both in collegiality and in beliefs about students, subject matter, and "good" practices.

COMMUNITIES OF PRACTICE IN ACADEMIC DEPARTMENTS

Substantive differences between professional communities inside the high schools we studied shape how teachers construct practice for the same or similar students. We found that academic departments constitute important contexts for high school teaching—as distinctive subject cultures and sometimes as communities of practice.[2] Most academic departments in the schools we studied lack a strong technical culture, or shared ideas about teaching and learning, and show little "department effect" other than bounding subject cultures and identities. Teachers act independently and communicate little with department colleagues about their teaching (Johnson 1990; Siskin 1994).

In high school departments where we found strong technical cultures, we saw that the substance of shared vision and norms for classroom practice ranged from teacher-centered, traditional practice to student-centered, innovative practice. Most intriguing in light of the lack of attention researchers pay to departments, we found instances where principles of department technical cultures differ substantively within the same high school. Moreover, survey data for teachers in comprehensive high schools show that departments, and not schools, are the locus of technical culture and source of considerable variation in teachers' expectations for their students' academic achievement.[3] Our cases elaborate how these department-level differences create fundamentally different settings for teaching and learning—even within the same school.

Strong and Weak Departments Side by Side
The English and social studies departments at Oak Valley High School exemplify how two different academic departments can form fundamentally different contexts for teaching and learning in the same school. According to teachers' survey responses, Oak Valley's English department has the strongest technical culture of any department in our sample while the same school's social studies department ranks among the weakest.[4] Since all Oak Valley students take classes in both departments, the objective student context for teachers in both departments is the same. The departments are located steps away from one another. Yet their cultures are worlds apart in terms of expectations for student learning and beliefs about effective teaching practice.

The English department, home to approximately twenty-five teachers, has an express and shared vision: they want their teaching to support all students with quality instruction. The department chair told us: "The kids are the reason we are here—content is really important, and so is being fair to students in terms of consistent instructional quality and evaluation. We're professionals, and people really care here."

Oak Valley's English teachers agree on the importance of all students succeeding, whether they are high achievers or indifferent to academic work. How individual faculty members go about supporting that student success is left to the discretion of each teacher. In fact, the English department embraces a range of pedagogical persuasions, as its chair describes it, from "really open and nondirective, to pretty traditional." He estimates that about a third of the faculty adheres to the "straightforward old style—where you do the reading and you answer these questions and you do this vocabulary and you do these worksheets kind of thing." "You are really open to do what methods you want," explained a department newcomer, as long as it works for students.

A tour of a morning's English classes underscores the variety of teaching styles within the department as well as the department's strong student focus. In a first-period British literature class, the teacher probes her students' understanding of the previous night's reading assignment. Out in one of the portable classrooms, a writing teacher plays classical music on a boom box while students work in small groups critiquing each other's writing. He holds individual conferences with students in a corner of the room, asking questions about their intent, suggesting ways to strengthen their argument, pointing to the work of another student as an example of a more effective writing strategy. Two Advanced Placement courses, taught in the same period by different teachers, reflect the range of department styles. One course is taught "pretty much to the test," the teacher said. "It's not a gruel-a-thon, but there is a lot of reading and writing." Ken, next door, teaches AP more like a college seminar. "You know, it's just a different philosophy," he said. Some English teachers stress writing as process; others are more comfortable with a strong literature-based approach. Department norms reject a "one right way" conception of practice and support individual teacher preferences, just as they respect differences in students' learning styles. According to the department chair, "[Regardless of classroom style,] the overall feeling is the kids are the ones that need to be doing, who are in it, and [instruction] should actively involve them." The English department sees all of its students as learners; the faculty is responsible for creating classroom contexts in which they can succeed.

The social studies department's vision of classroom teaching, as expressed by the chair, derives from traditional subject-area norms and ideas about the ways teachers have taught for generations. Expectations for its students assume high levels of attention, compliance, and focus. For example, exasperated by her students' inability to recall the meaning of "social contract," the chair derided their motivation and commitment to learning and revealed her own investment in teacher-directed instruction. "Today's newspaper mentioned social contract, and I asked them what that meant. It wasn't until sixth period that someone was able to tell me 'John Locke.' I had drilled them in John Locke and told them not to forget. You're trying to teach, but they don't want to learn . . . there's terrible resistance."

❧❧❧

These divergent cultures of high school teaching practice reflect the departments' widely differing norms of professional community. The English department, as figure 3.1 displays, is a highly collegial community where teachers' relationships extend well beyond congeniality to collaboration and out-of-school lives. This department illustrates how the immediate professional community engenders a particular teaching culture. English teachers meet regularly to share writing, discuss student work, and work on curriculum. They eat lunch together; talk quickly turns to "how'd your morning go?" and discussions of classroom surprises, highs, or problems. They get together socially as well. "This department is very close," explained a teacher who has taught at Oak Valley for more than a decade.

Teachers' shared commitment to ensuring all students' academic success support traditions of sharing and professional equity in the English department's culture. Individual knowledge and experiences function as a resource for the entire English faculty, as members of the department regularly swap materials, ideas, and courses. A veteran told us:

It's everyday practice that teachers are handing [out]—sample lessons they've done, or an assignment that they've tried,

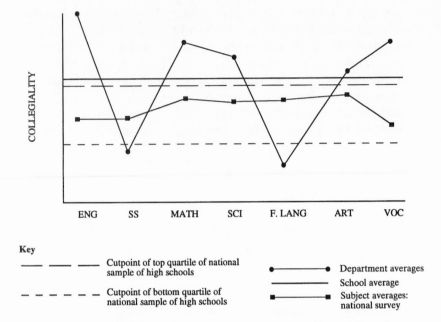

Key

—— —— —— Cutpoint of top quartile of national
sample of high schools

— — — — — Cutpoint of bottom quartile of
national sample of high schools

●————● Department averages

———— School average

■————■ Subject averages:
national survey

Figure 3.1 Department Differences in Teacher Collegiality: Oak Valley
High School

NOTE: This analysis uses a survey scale measuring teacher collegiality, or strength of
community (see appendix C for items that make up the collegiality scale). The figure
shows the overall school average score on collegiality, average scores for teachers in
seven different subject-area departments within the school, and national norms for
the respective subject areas (based on "High School and Beyond" survey data for
teachers classified according to their primary subject assignment). Data are for 121
Oak Valley teachers in these departments.

and [discussed] when it worked, [or] how they would do it differently. Or a new teacher joins the staff and instantly they
are paired up with a couple of buddies . . . and file drawers
and computer disks and everything are just made readily
available.

They just say, "Hey! I need some help." Especially when
you feel [like you're] floundering, which you do often. . . .
We really can turn to each other when something isn't working and say, "I need some help." I have heard of departments
where you have to watch your reputation and stuff, but that's
not the case here.

Oak Valley English teachers agree on the need to adapt and change their classroom practices and underscore the importance of collegial feedback and support to that process. Avoiding prescriptions of "best practices," the department supports each of its members to think through ways to reach all of their students in different courses and to reinvent practice according to their best judgment. Sharing and collaboration follow and support teachers' innovations in their classrooms. In the department's portion of their school's program quality review, we found this description: "Our department shares methods, materials, lesson plans, successes and struggles. We like each other and we draw on each others' strength and support."

In contrast, the social studies department comprises a roster of individuals, not a community of practice. In this weak department community, each teacher practices in isolation and is on his or her own to seek resources, respond to crises, or consider different ways of doing things. The teachers worry alone about their classrooms, and many are, as one told us, "losing sleep at night. There's absolutely no doubt about it. [Unpredictability associated with today's students] keeps those juices in your stomach churning." Teachers speak of "my materials" or "my course," but never mention their colleagues as resources—or even in positive terms.

These differences in professional community affect how Oak Valley English and social studies teachers connect students and subject matter—how they understand the parameters of the classroom triangle and what learning opportunities they develop for their students. Oak Valley's English department stands better equipped on multiple dimensions to work effectively with all students, both traditional and nontraditional. According to the chair, the department's policy of course rotation means that weak students can have "dynamite teachers." The department's strong norms of professional interdependence mean that every English teacher can respond to classroom challenges and anticipate new ones with an expanded repertoire. The faculty's distributed expertise serves all students, including students who do not fit the usual patterns. Experimentation and critical reflection are the norm and are supported by the close professional community. "One of the things I really like about this department is that people encourage you to try things," a teacher told us. "Personally, I'd rather have a grand failure than a very boring success. You try something different, get the kid interested." Ironically, many of the English department's strongest teachers (including the chair) find Advanced Placement courses their least preferred assignment because established course content and structure constrain their ability to innovate or engage students in serious problem-solving activities.

Perhaps it is not surprising that teachers in these two departments see the same students in very different terms. Oak Valley English teachers' comments are uniformly positive: "We have excellent students, cooperative, and there's good rapport with the teachers," said a former department chair. English teachers look to their practice as they consider why a lesson or class did not meet expectations for student accomplishment. Their attitude is to go back to the drawing board, confer with a colleague, try something different, institute new procedures that can better support all students. The chair described his new policy to "catch the ones who fall through the cracks":

> I call it the "intensive care list." After first semester, we
> make up a [confidential] list of students who aren't doing so
> well . . . it would send up a little flag, because sometimes it
> could take six weeks [into the next semester for grades to be
> sent to the department] and a progress list made up to find
> out who's in trouble. This [procedure] has just heightened
> communication and sharing [in the department]—you know,
> what worked, what didn't work, because these tend to be
> hard-core cases.

Student success is explicitly everyone's responsibility in the English department.

Social studies teachers construct a very different classroom ethos and hold different ideas about students and why their performance often falls short of expectations. Social studies teachers describe disappointing classroom outcomes primarily in students' attitudes about learning. One said, "The kids—there's no quest for knowledge. Not all, but that's in general . . . it's not important to them. They just don't want to learn." An economics teacher, worrying about a rash of failing grades recalled "more of a bell-shaped curve" in prior years' student performance and concluded, "I really can't think that the material is causing the problem [since it was the same], but rather that the individuals involved are either motivated to learn it or not." (This comment echoes the Valley High School math teacher's assertion that the problem is "with the kid, not the curriculum.")

Comments from social studies teachers also reflect reliance on subject-matter orthodoxy. Oak Valley's department, like social studies departments throughout California and the country, struggled with implications of new curriculum frameworks and standards for history and social studies. Even after two years of meetings, they have been unable to agree on a department view of social studies, or even on an approach to the California framework. The chair vocalized her dislike of changes prompted by this curriculum reform, and her strategy for retaining traditions:

> I'm really concerned about this dumping of Western civ. How do you know where you're going if you don't know where you've been? All of that is our heritage. My kids read *The Prince* the other day. Now if you dump that, then how do you begin to understand certain things about the rise of dictators? And I thought as I was putting that unit together, "Am I wasting my time because we are not going to use it in the [new] curriculum?" I thought, "No! Under totalitarianism! I can still use this!"

Old ideas often undermine "new" ones in this department. This teacher and others in the social studies department talk about "always wanting to try new things," but conventional ideas of text and materials strangle the concepts of change and new practice that follow. Oak Valley's social studies teachers have little to challenge the logic of subject-area traditions of "good student" and "good practice," and so they reflect the norms of "individualism" and "conservatism" that Dan Lortie (1975) describes as typical of schoolteaching.

These norms also embrace established ideas of teacher-directed classrooms and passive student roles. For example, the social studies chair related a classroom incident that she felt signaled students' personal and professional disrespect. A student criticized her requirement that the students keep "point charts—so they always know where they are in my class." During the confrontation that followed, the chair had insisted, "It's not an option. When you've got as much education, as much time in the classroom as I have, they [have no place to] tell me how to teach."

Social studies teachers are more likely than their colleagues in the English department to view their job as routine, while English teachers are more inclined to put students at the center and to adapt their practices to accommodate students. These differences are not subject-based, but are rooted in department culture. Most important from a student's perspective, the very same students whom English teachers see as bright, interesting, and energetic, social studies teachers see as apathetic, ill-prepared, and unwilling to work hard.[5]

The same students receive radically different messages from one period to the next. A freshman, for example, who was assigned to skills classes in language and social studies, receives praise from his first-period English teacher for his forceful writing and encouragement to move to the "regular" track next semester, only to hear in his second-period social studies class that he is probably "overachieving in here," and would certainly have problems if he moved from remedial course.

English teachers at Oak Valley experience a much greater degree of professional autonomy and control than do their social studies colleagues across the hall. The English teachers understand choices about teaching and learning to be theirs, and also assess their success or disappointments in those terms. Conversely, the social studies teachers look outside their classrooms to explain poor student outcomes and their own dissatisfaction. They cite such factors as student decline, subject-matter orthodoxy, the bureaucracy to justify the choices they make in their practice and to explain the frustration they experience, blaming "what the 'authorities' (quote-unquote) deem proper classroom activities," as the economics teacher put it.[6]

This tale of two departments underscores the power of professional culture and community in constructing the everyday classroom contexts for students and teachers. These cases show how, for example, "autonomy" can assume different meanings in different professional communities. In the social studies department, autonomy means isolation and reinforces norms of individualism and conservatism. In the English department, professional autonomy and strong community are mutually reinforcing, rather than oppositional. Here collegial support and interaction enable individual teachers to reconsider and revise their classroom practice confidently because department norms are mutually negotiated and understood. The collegial environment of this department enables teachers to use professional discretion to make choices, within student-focused values and norms of practice. Without question, Peggy Sue would find support in the English department; she might well find herself on the department's "intensive care list" and the focus of special effort. Across the hall in social studies, however, she would likely be dismissed as "not interested in learning" and typical of the poor academic attitudes exhibited by "kids today."

The Same Subject: Two Departments

Differences in professional culture between the two Oak Valley departments are striking because they share exactly the same students and policy environments. However, they differ in subject contexts. Could this partly account for the differences we found? While our data reveal no systematic differences in predispositions of English and social studies teachers to adapt teaching to their students, we do find significant differences between mathematics and other subjects as a cultural context of teaching. The particular constraints on teaching framed by mathematics education culture make it a particularly interesting subject context for investigating communities of practice.

Subject cultures of teaching. Most high school teachers in our sample see their subject area as a critical context and a defining factor in their professional identity. Teachers speak of their subject area as having norms for how to teach, as well as direction for content to be covered and student learning goals. They understand their subject domain as largely determining how and what they teach.

All high school subjects are not "equal" in terms of the constraints or opportunities they provide teachers to adapt practice or change routines. Subject-based constraints on adapting practice to nontraditional students derive from the disciplines' materials, practices, and beliefs. Subjects and courses that rely heavily on written documents, for instance, frame more difficult challenges for engaging students with limited proficiency in English or low levels of literacy in any language. Close readings of Shakespeare's plays or historical documents fall outside the capacity of many such students. Subjects like science or drama that include long-term projects are difficult to adapt to high rates of student mobility and absence common in poor urban schools.

Subjects with traditions of high "sequential dependence"— the progressive order of course topics, concepts, and skills— such as mathematics and foreign languages, prompt teachers to emphasize students' "readiness" to move from on course to another. They express frustration at the "missing steps" in many students' learning, or at students' failure to acquire the basic skills thought necessary to move to the next level of instruction. Many contemporary students' high levels of mobility or poor attendance particularly bother teachers who see the content of their subject as highly sequential. "One third of my class is absent on any given day," sighed a California math teacher. "The problem for me is that it is a different third! How am I supposed to teach?"

Several teachers point to this aspect of their subject matter as a reason why students are discouraged in their classes and find it harder to do well. For instance, a college preparatory math teacher told us, "In history or English, kids can understand the material more easily. In math, there is an initial level you have to get to before you understand it at all; until you get that first understanding, there is a big nothing. This is why kids get frustrated. They don't feel that way in history. These subject-area differences are why history teachers don't get bad PR like math teachers do."

In contrast to the subject-specific rigidity expressed by many math teachers, an English teacher remarked on the relative freedom she has in selecting texts for her eleventh-grade literature class: "As long as I cover the core pieces in the district curriculum, I can choose what I think my kids will enjoy. It is a little different every year, depending on who my kids are and what I am excited about at the moment."

Accordingly, we found that math teachers are significantly

more likely than are teachers of English, social studies, or science to see their subject matter as static and their job as routine.[7] Science, English, and social studies teachers generally view their fields as changing continually, generating new knowledge, theories, and perspectives. In contrast, math and foreign-language teachers tend to see their subject as relatively constant or static, with content changing little from year to year. Math teachers, especially, feel that much of their instruction is predetermined. As a Michigan teacher put it: "The district's math program leads you down the straight and narrow."

Subject domains operate as an important context for teaching, in short, because they carry cultural mandates for teaching practice. Subject areas differ in their conceptions of "good" teaching and the constraints teachers perceive on their freedom to select materials, pedagogy, and instructional objectives. Math teachers, more than teachers of other academic subjects, feel constrained by canons of subject-area culture and demands for curriculum coverage. In mathematics classes, then, one would expect to see the "same" general content and pedagogy, regardless of student or organizational context, as math teachers pursue traditional norms of practice. For these reasons, mathematics represents a "worst case" in terms of teachers' potential openness to rethinking traditional assumptions or developing new practices to engage nontraditional students in the discipline.

Two neighboring mathematics departments in our sample—Esperanza and Rancho—illustrate the power of teacher communities to establish norms of practice; these Mostaza district math faculties have constructed radically different cultures of teaching within the same, constrained subject context. Oak Valley's English and social studies departments show how "school" can mean very different things to teachers and students moving through the same school day in the same school building, depending on how teacher communities understand and craft their jobs and responsibilities. Similarly, these cases of contrasting mathematics departments show how "subject," as understood and conveyed to students, assumes substantively different meanings, depending on the culture of the professional community in which teachers teach.

Contrasting math department communities. Math teachers at Esperanza and Rancho High Schools work only a few miles from each other in the Mostaza Unified School District. They teach the same blend of students—a diverse population of recently arrived immigrants from Asia, the Middle East, Africa, Mexico, and South America, as well as resident Hispanic students who participate in the district's desegregation program. The desegregation program brings minority students from all over Mostaza in fleets of buses; white students from the neighborhood make up the minority in each school.

Each school experienced rapid change in student demographics beginning in 1987 as the district's court order was implemented (see appendix B for a description of the Mostaza district). At both Rancho and Esperanza, the student body changed from predominately middle-class and white to "majority minority" in the space of a year. The mathematics departments at Rancho and Esperanza responded in fundamentally different ways to their new students. Rancho teachers generally "kept traditions" and failed students who did not perform in their conventional classrooms; Esperanza's math teachers reinvented mathematics to support students' learning in new ways.[8]

Rancho's math department operates according to established subject-matter conventions. While it offers a full range of classes for its student population of sixteen hundred, students are highly tracked and must pass minimum competency tests to advance to a higher level. The faculty's hierarchical subject-matter assumptions are evident in its response to a district mandate to collapse the multilayered remedial courses into one state-designed course (Math A). Rancho math teachers looked for ways to circumvent this "latest" district attempt at curriculum standardization: "We think there are three levels of kids in this school below Algebra 1, and most people don't want to believe that. There's some thought afoot to put all kids below Algebra 1 in one class, meaning Math A class. And we're already seeing this year that if we were to do that, at least 70 percent, 80 percent would fail. No doubt about it." Rancho math teachers also recognized that they and the students would suffer as a result: "Nobody wants to admit that when we bring in six hundred ninth-graders there's going to be a huge number that aren't ready for this level of attention to detail. There aren't any places for them. So I don't know what's going to happen, aside from the fact that they're just going to have a miserable year and fail, I'll have a miserable year, the kids that are okay will have a miserable year, everything's miserable."

Teachers in this department actively resisted pressures to adjust their practices and curriculum. After offering Math A for one year, Rancho math teachers abandoned it and instead provided remedial students a watered-down version of Algebra 1/2. This course, normally a one-year sequence, became a two-year sequence of Algebra 1A/1B and Algebra 2A/2B. The department relied on standardized, multiple-choice tests to determine students' math "readiness." Students' failure on them was explained to us in terms of poor student attitudes. In one teacher's opinion, "For someone who knows how to study, how could you not pass? Probably what's missing is the motivation to do the preparation so that they can pass, which could mean just a set of notes. This is not what's between the ears."

Whereas the Rancho faculty held students back until they could demonstrate readiness to move to the next level, the Esperanza math department organized itself to advance all students through mathematics, including calculus. The Esperanza math department was founded on a strong commitment to students and the belief that students and teachers alike could move through the math curriculum. At the minimum, Esperanza math teachers expected their students to enroll in algebra. Contrary to the hurdles erected by department policy at Rancho, Esperanza math teachers removed layers of remedial classes these students would have to pass in order to enroll in "Introduction to Algebra." One teacher said: "We recommend, beg, plead, and coerce, and everything else, to get them to take algebra. Because we're trying to build that up. We have a new policy at this school where no student takes anything lower than 'Introduction to Algebra.'"

Esperanza's math teachers discovered that the rethinking they had to do in light of their new students was fundamental to their content domain. For example, one teacher described how she discarded her hierarchical conceptions of mathematics to emphasize ideas instead:

We used to have a basic math lab, and what we found out is the same thing that people are finding out everywhere . . . kids have done fractions for five years, they could care less about doing fractions—so why don't we do something with them? And I've always given my real low-level kids multiplication tables so that they can do fractions, calculators so that they can do decimals, and, it's not that they shouldn't have these skills, but just because you haven't learned your multiplication tables doesn't mean you *cannot* do fractions. So, you know, maybe with luck they'll learn them both.

A colleague echoed her disdain for a sequential skills-building view of math: "I hear a lot of people say, 'I can't let this kid go on, he doesn't know his times tables.' I say to hell with it, let's give him a calculator and get on with it and let him *think!*"

Department members work hard to provide opportunities for students to advance to higher-level classes. The chair told us: "The last few years we seem to retain our kids [in mathematics classes through graduation] pretty well here at Esperanza, and I think it's because our teachers . . . really bend over backwards to encourage kids and motivate kids. . . . [For example,] we still have two calculus classes. For a school our size, we're around twelve-hundred-plus students, we're still able to maintain two calculus classes."

The department intentionally built its instructional capacity in much the same way as did Oak Valley's English department, rotating teachers through all of the courses. The chair said that "everyone is willing to take their turn with the lower [classes]. We've tried to foster that attitude throughout the years and so far it's held."

Esperanza math faculty reinvent practice to accommodate students' learning styles, uneven math backgrounds, and often precarious personal lives. But they do not water down, "dumb down," or otherwise compromise content. Their students' accomplishments and high levels of math enrollment testify to the effectiveness of this math department's efforts. A teacher said:

Maybe we're not doing all we could for the most outstanding students, but usually they're pretty well motivated and make up the difference themselves. I think we're doing a lot more for the average students and below-average students because we have math teachers at every level. And . . . if you look at our [California Assessment Program] scores last year—for an integrated student body with a 55 percent minority, which Brookvale and Rancho all have, we are head and shoulders [above them in student achievement scores]. In our [state-wide, stratified by school type] control group we were 99 percentile, 86 [percentile] overall in math. We felt [our effort] showed, we feel we're on the right track.

Student enrollment choices also testify to the success of this department in working with all students. "It may look chaotic to an outsider," explained a teacher, "but as long as we are having the success we are . . . We have an unbelievable math enrollment in this school. I don't think you'll find any school with [almost] thirteen hundred kids [and] with eleven hundred taking math."

TEACHING AND LEARNING IN HIGH SCHOOL
PROFESSIONAL COMMUNITIES

American teachers confront a fundamental challenge to traditional ideas about "good teaching" and "good students" as they enter classrooms marked by extraordinary student diversity, find themselves accountable to a new array of standards and frameworks, and wrestle with the avalanche of issues that plague public education today. For the most part, they have responded by clinging tenaciously to the canons and taken-for-granteds of teaching. (Recall that approximately three-quarters of the teachers in our sample of typical secondary schools rated themselves high on "traditional" teaching roles and expectations for practice.) In some high school settings, like Rancho's math department, teacher communities have developed strong norms and structures of practice to enforce pedagogical traditions in their discipline and to organize learning opportunities for their diverse students that differ in academic purpose and teaching quality.

In some schools and departments, however, teachers are questioning traditions of practice and designing course content and teaching strategies to engage all their students in serious

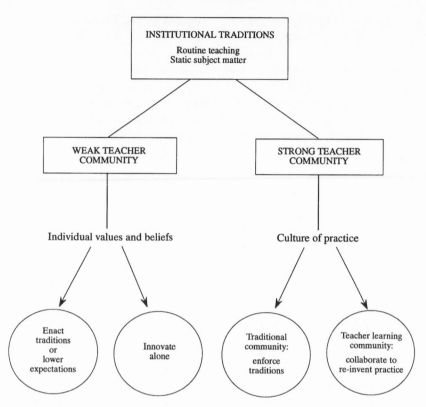

Figure 3.2 How Teacher Communities Mediate Institutional Traditions in Teaching

academic learning. These communities of practice appear to do better for most students than those heavily invested in maintaining traditional teaching standards and those with weak technical cultures.

Our case examples of types of teacher communities show that *how* traditions in teaching play out in the classroom depends on the strength and character of the professional community through which they move. Figure 3.2 represents the alternate ways in which teacher professional communities mediate taken-for-granted traditions of teaching—routine teacher-centered pedagogy, static bodies of subject knowledge, receptive student roles—to construct distinctive communities of teaching practice. Teacher communities differ in strength of mission, that is, in whether or to what degree shared goals and values support a sense of community.

Weak teacher communities, such as the social studies department in Oak Valley High School, are essentially "pass-through" environments. Department expectations, norms, or conversation do not prompt teachers to question their assumptions about good practice and response to their nontraditional students' poor performance, or to consider new ways of schoolteaching. Strong teacher communities like the math departments in Esperanza and Rancho High Schools constitute communities of practice—professional communities in which teachers share a sense of common mission and negotiate principles, policies, and resources for their practice. Contrary to conventional wisdom regarding the positive role that strong school community has on student outcomes, we found that strong communities do not uniformly support teachers' and students' success; indeed, some establish highly unequal learning opportunities for their students.

The strong communities of practice we studied constitute substantively different settings for teachers' and students' work and success. They differ in their cultures of practice, focused alternatively on conserving traditions or innovating. In Rancho's math department's traditional communities of practice, teachers are united in support of established canons of discipline instruction and consider that high rates of student failure signal their department's high academic standards. In learning communities like Esperanza's math department, teachers collaborate to design new practices that engage their students' in mathematics.

In all schools and departments, we found individual teachers who were learning and working to improve their practice, especially in Paloma, where keeping up in one's discipline was a job expectation and teachers were highly active professionally. However, what distinguishes teacher learning communities from other school settings is their collective stance on learning in the context of shared work and responsibilities. In such communities, teachers together address the challenges of their student body and explore ways of improving practice to advance learning. This collective inquiry generates knowledge *of* practice, while a teacher's individual learning in strong traditional communities draws upon knowledge *for* practice, derived from research and theory outside the teaching setting.[9]

Both traditional communities and teacher learning communities are distinguished from weak and strong collegial communities by their focus on teaching and learning and their collective approach to organizing practice. Yet their cultures of practice diverge in beliefs about content, learning, good teaching, and effective colleague relationships.

◂◂◂

Students' learning experiences in high schools or departments with weak teaching cultures are akin to an instructional lottery, in which their learning opportunities depend heavily on which teachers they draw, from class to class and year to year. Individual teachers' preferences and beliefs about students and subject matter define students' classroom experiences, ranging from strict adherence to curriculum coverage and standardized testing, to "dumbed-down" content, to collective work on challenging problems and issues in a subject.

A strong school or department culture of teaching minimizes the classroom lottery for students, for better or worse. In Rancho's math department, struggling students fail and thus reinforce teachers' beliefs that they are "just not up to" standards. Virtually the same students encounter a different educational world in the supportive culture of Esperanza's math department, where student difficulties are considered to be a problem for content pedagogy, rather than a problem of student deficiencies.

The Oak Valley freshman enrolled in skills classes experiences daily the significance of his teachers' professional communities as he moves from his engaging, student-centered English class to his dreary social studies class the next period. As he progresses from grade to grade in the school, he can count on support for learning in all of his English classes, but his fate in social studies will depend on his class assignments. Will he end up with the department chair and struggle to engage her rigid and narrow view of history? Will he draw the economics teacher always trying to foster his students' critical thinking? Or will he, as a low-track student, be assigned to one of the teachers whom the chair called the department's "embarrassments," who manage their classes with worksheets and "seatwork"?

Professional communities in today's high schools differ in

strength and in their cultures of practice—differences that matter profoundly for teaching and learning. We step back from considerations of teaching cultures to examine how teachers' work and careers are organized in different communities. In what ways do these teacher communities constitute "policy systems" for teaching? How do teachers construe and experience their professional rewards and their careers in teaching within the distinctive kinds of professional community?

CHAPTER 4

Communities and Teaching Careers

Teachers here in the English department especially are very generous in the sharing of information and actually reach out to colleagues. In other schools, some teachers are very protective of their territory, or there's a competitive nature in teaching. It's not true here.

In the department it's standard, everyday practice that teachers are handing other teachers sample lessons that they've done or an assignment that they tried, or a new teacher joins the staff and instantly they're paired up with a couple of buddies who are teaching the same schedule. [This is] quite different from the other three schools where I've taught, where it seems that teachers did their own thing and you didn't really share.

We have a great department here. I have so many things going on for me in the classroom and outside the classroom that keep me young professionally.

This is how three teachers describe their professional lives and careers in the collaborative Oak Valley English department. In contrast, teaching in Oak Valley's social studies department is private and conducive to frustration and professional disengagement, as two other teachers make clear:

You need a certain amount of professional pride and confidence that you're doing something that is worthwhile [to keep engaged]. In a lot of ways, we're not given credit for the work that we do. My primary job is not raising kids. But yet I think that we're getting an awful lot of pressure to do that. And I resent that.

Sometimes I think I need to get out of the classroom to go into some other area of education, otherwise I'm not sure how much longer I'll last. I'm having to do it [revise my American history course] pulling on my own resources and doing it myself. And that's frustrating. . . . If anything drives me out of the classroom more than anything else, it's the disrespect for teaching. And the kids—there's no quest for knowledge . . . I don't think people consider us professionals.

Teachers' talk about their jobs in Oak Valley High School reveals striking differences in their departments' collegial norms and the professional rewards they engender. English teachers rave about their relations with colleagues and their policy of assigning courses so that beginning teachers are supported. Social studies teachers complain about their colleagues, about courses needing revision, and about not getting credit for their hard work with today's students. In describing their work lives, these Oak Valley teachers convey radically different experiences of their careers in the same school and district—keeping "young professionally" in one department; in the other, losing "professional pride and respect" and needing to "get out of the classroom."

Anchoring these career experiences are teachers' relationships with colleagues and understanding of the core facets of teaching practice highlighted in chapter 3—their students and subjects.

TEACHING CAREER ANCHORS

Colleagues

Students ——————— Courses

These referents are not the ones that social scientists consider when they describe the teaching career. They look instead to formal structures, such as occupational levels and job promotion systems, and find American schoolteachers' careers to be "flat" (Lortie 1975). The teaching profession generally lacks formal structures for career advancement, apart from district pay scales that grade salaries according to teachers' seniority, education, and credentials.[1] Social science theory and teaching policy that frame career in structural terms miss important sources of high school teachers' professional rewards—the quality of their relations with students, courses, and colleagues. We take "career" as the experience of these rewards over time. Teachers in the same system experience their careers in radically different ways—as advancing, as stagnating, or as declining—depending on the trend of these core, informal professional rewards.

High school teachers' careers, like their classroom practices, mirror the culture of their professional communities. We found that the strong high school and department communities of practice portrayed in chapter 3 had distinctive career cultures that expressed and set conditions for patterns of classroom practice. The notion of "career culture" refers to teachers' shared understandings and expectations for relations with colleagues, teaching assignments, and professional rewards. These cultures are important because they mediate teachers' opportunities for intrinsic professional rewards, which Dan Lortie (1975) and others have shown to be primary in teaching. Intrinsic rewards of teaching include satisfying relationships with colleagues and growth in one's subject area, as well as success in promoting students' learning. We found that teachers' experiences of these rewards, and their sense of career advancement, vary significantly between the high schools and subject departments within them.

High school professional communities can afford teachers more rewarding or less rewarding collegial relationships—mutual respect and interactions based in shared commitments to a school mission, to subject discipline, to common students. They can offer many or few opportunities or for teachers to teach and grow in their subject area—access to courses that fit a teacher's preparation and interests. And most fundamentally, they can contribute much or little to teachers' success in engaging their students in challenging content and in school.

Teachers' experience of rise or fall in any or all of these professional rewards over time can feel like job mobility, analogous to a promotion or demotion in a formal career system. The patterns we found in teachers' career experiences were closely connected to conditions of their work in particular high schools and subject departments.

PATTERNS OF HIGH SCHOOL TEACHERS' WORK LIVES AND CAREERS

Teachers' work lives and career experiences differ across the three kinds of department and school professional communities we have defined in our sample—weak communities, strong traditional communities of practice, and teacher learning communities. Distinguishing them are norms of collegiality and job assignments: whether teachers keep their practice private and follow seniority rules for teaching assignments, or coordinate to ensure a fit between teacher expertise and course tracks, or collaborate on instruction and share teaching assignments across the curriculum. These alternative ways in which high school teachers work together in a subject department or school community shape their opportunities for success with students and the nature of professional rewards and careers they experience over time.

Privacy Norms and Declining Career Rewards

As in the schools where Dan Lortie's teachers taught in the 1960s, a "privacy norm" governs collegial relations in typical high schools today. In these settings, teachers talk about anything but their practice; being a "good colleague" means not asking for, or giving, advice about classroom practice. Relationships among the Oak Valley social studies teachers are like that, as they are in most departments in the comprehensive high schools we studied. Whatever pride in professional autonomy teachers may take from this condition, most feel isolated in their work and frustrated by the lack of support they get from their colleagues. Special conditions in high school teaching may engender professional isolation beyond the broader norm in American education that Lortie observed. For one, the departmental organization of comprehensive high schools fragments the larger school social system and makes teachers more dependent on the particular group of colleagues in their discipline. Second, the notion that high school teachers are subject "experts" may especially inhibit their seeking knowledge and advice from one another.

Privacy norms and conditions of isolation in high schools appear to be self-perpetuating: when teachers feel that their colleagues are not sharing resources and experience, they become protective of their own resources and successes. When teachers do not share work, they tend to see their efforts in proprietary terms. The Oak Valley social studies teacher who revised the American history course by "pulling on my own resources and doing it myself," for example, does not feel generous toward the colleagues who failed to help. She complained: "You get tired of sharing and getting nothing back. . . . Suddenly you begin to retrench and say 'Wait a minute,' you know." In this anomic department culture, a norm of protectiveness characterizes collegial relations.

Teachers' experience of professional isolation is not endemic to high school communities where practice is private. The exceptions in our sample were in private college preparatory schools, especially Paloma, where collegiality centers on the school's mission, where teachers are highly engaged in their disciplines, and where students are academically successful. Teachers in such schools prize the opportunity to create courses around their special expertise and interests and to teach as they wish. A Paloma teacher expressed her sense of privilege in such privacy of practice: "No one interferes with you, and the administration always backs their teachers." The strong academic mission of these schools creates a sense of community, and teachers feel that they share in a schoolwide enterprise, sponsoring their students into elite segments of the higher education system.

Teachers' rewards in weak professional communities depend especially on what courses and students they are assigned. In typical public high schools, union-negotiated contracts establish a seniority rule for teachers' job assignments, and the most experienced teachers get "first dibs" on job openings for which they are generally qualified. In regions where population patterns create a downward enrollment trend, as they did during the late 1990s in the Michigan districts we studied, seniority-based assignments mean that new high school teachers often teach out of the subject and grade for which they were prepared and that they are uncertain from year to year whether they will have a teaching job or will need to find a new occupation.[2]

Seniority prerogatives also affect teachers' options on course assignments within their primary subject department. A young physics teacher recently hired to teach science in California's Onyx Ridge High School confided to us that her only hope of teaching physics there in the next ten years was if the department's senior physics teacher died, since she was sure that he would never leave the school. The veteran Onyx Ridge English department chair reserves high-track classes for herself, even though the principal considers her to be weak and her reputation with students is abysmal.

The sink-or-swim conditions of beginning one's teaching career in such high school settings appear to be customary in U.S. education and are defended by the notion that new teachers should "pay their dues." Not only are beginning teachers assigned to the least desirable courses, often out of their main field of preparation, but they are unsupported by colleagues in weak high school communities. The Oak Valley social studies department chair even derided her inexperienced colleagues so assigned: "They don't know how to do anything besides just take the text and use the teachers' guide. They have no idea how to go about finding materials. They are so insecure about teaching that they are afraid to try anything new." No wonder that teachers in such communities often feel isolated, frustrated, and resentful of both their colleagues and their students.

Professional rewards are sparse in weak high school communities. While veteran teachers are positioned to realize the intrinsic rewards that come from teaching classes of academically oriented students,[3] teachers in these communities also seem most concerned over markers of professional status. One source of status rewards and prerogatives is the subjects they teach. Academic teachers are accorded higher professional status than their colleagues teaching nonacademic subjects (Little 1993), and mathematics and science teachers have the highest status and most clout in their schools. As our colleague Leslie Siskin documented in her study of Michigan's Highlander School and California's Rancho and Oak Valley High Schools, math and science come out "on top" of the discipline hierarchy for several reasons—their higher value in American society and in education reform, the scarcity of subject specialists in teaching, the authority and agency of their formalized disciplines, and (for science) the material investments they command (Siskin 1994, 124–32). The academic status of a subject confers prestige to teachers on a zero-sum basis and therefore assigns low prestige to some groups of teachers. Yet even at the top of the status order, academic prestige and prerogatives have a limited ability to sustain more general professional commitment.

Teachers in weak high school settings often focus on their students' academic and social status as a sign of their own professional status and career success.[4] In both Michigan and California urban high schools, many teachers talk about changes in their students' characteristics in language that conveys a sense of decline. Michigan teachers talk about having lost "good kids," "good students," when the economy suffered and middle-class families left the inner-city neighborhoods. Teachers in California's Mostaza district talk nostalgically about the days before court-ordered desegregation brought an abrupt shift in their students' social and academic status. In the past, these teachers had taken pride in serving the offspring of middle-class families, bound for college and professional careers; some of them now feel a sense of loss, that they have been diminished professionally by serving the children of very poor and poorly educated families. Some complain, further, that they are unfairly being held accountable for the mounting social and economic problems of today's youth and experience criticism of public education as professionally and personally demeaning. One Michigan teacher commented: "I don't tell people I'm a teacher anymore."

Teachers in high schools that lack strong communities of practice, and that have growing proportions of nontraditional students, generally experience decline in their professional rewards. The downward trend in their teaching career prompts many teachers to withdraw from the profession, either by disengaging or by leaving for another occupation.

Stratifying Norms and Career Inequality

High school communities that uphold traditional practice, such as Rancho's math department, engender a different pattern in teachers' day-to-day work and overall career. In these communities, teachers' relationships and work organization follow the logic of their classroom practice—learning is sequential, skills are ordered, and readiness to learn particular subject matter is unequal. Teachers' work is organized around a tracking system, structured according to students' academic proficiency levels.

Teachers' relations with one another are neither private nor collaborative in these communities. Rather, collegial relations focus on coordinating students' passages through course ladders—developing tests, reviewing results for student placement, and adapting the course schedule to match student performance distributions. In the elite private schools, less attention is placed on school-based tests for tracking, and more emphasis is placed on external assessments such as AP exams. Teachers play specialized and unequal roles in the organization according to their kind and level of subject expertise. This division of labor makes it uncommon for teachers to discuss their classroom practice, since they rarely share a course with another teacher in the department. The professional hierarchy sometimes plays out in unequal power and influence among teachers in such departments, when the more "advanced" teachers meet informally to make department decisions.

Teacher assignment practices in traditional department and school communities follow a logic of expertise—teachers' subject expertise is matched to students' competence in the subject. The best-prepared teachers are assigned to the most academically advanced students; the least-prepared teachers are assigned to the lowest-achieving students. Teachers are tracked, just as students are tracked. Teachers' shared beliefs about the importance of qualifications for filling course positions supplant seniority rules, in practice though not in official policy, by prompting teachers to chose or to accept their proper place in the curriculum.

Teacher tracking—or the practice of assigning teachers to mostly low-track or to mostly high-track classes—is not unique to the strong traditional departments and schools in our sample; it is simply exaggerated there.[5] High school tracking systems are institutionalized in American secondary education—with their "honors," "advanced," and Advanced Placement (AP) courses that carry certification through external testing and college recognition, on the top end, and "remedial," "basic," or "general" classes on the bottom. In the general status order of high school teaching, it is most prestigious to teach the "top" courses. However, as Merilee Finley (1982) found in her ethnographic study of high school English departments, not all teachers aspire to the top classes, though most try to avoid being assigned to the low-level academic courses, which are difficult and confer low professional status.

Further legitimizing teacher tracking practices in these professional communities is a broader market dynamic for teacher placement in American education that matches the best-qualified teachers with schools serving the most academically successful students.[6] For example, we saw how advantaged schools can bend seniority rules to recruit accomplished teachers. The principal of middle-class Onyx Ridge High School posted an English teaching position to fit the unique profile of a particular district teacher ready to bid for the job—qualifications including "a track record in teaching AP English literature and composition, advising yearbooks, and coaching women's soccer." Many Onyx Ridge teachers proudly told us that they were part of this "hand-picked faculty," considering their hiring as career advancement. In this traditional school community, most departments track teachers and consider this practice to be logical and fair.

Teachers low on the totem pole in such professional communities often feel marginal. Consider the experience of this young Onyx Ridge English teacher assigned to low-track classes in the department and committed to serving her students bused in from a poor district neighborhood:

My ideas don't have a place in this school. They do, I think, for some of my kids, not all, but for many of my kids. This campus chooses to see itself as an elite academic institution, as the smaller version of UC Adobe Viejo, as the "cream of the crop" school in Adobe Viejo. It does not perceive itself as a school that is here to meet student needs, particularly those that might be different from the upper-class community in which it is located. . . . So my talents, or my desires, or my skills don't have any place here. Is there something that encourages me to do what I do for my kids? No. It's from watching Jaime Escalante in *Stand and Deliver*. It's from my eleventh-grade English teacher, it's from my college experience when my professors pushed and pushed and pushed me. But it sure as heck isn't from anything I've gotten in [teaching in this professional community].

Because of her low-track courses and students, this teacher is marginalized in this strong traditional department and school community. She feels professionally isolated, unrewarded, and uncertain about her teaching career.

Teachers' opportunities for professional growth and progress are highly unequal in communities with this career pattern. Not only do high-track teachers reap intrinsic rewards that come from teaching academically engaged students, they are more esteemed by colleagues in and out of their schools. They are more influential in their departments and schools and better able to pursue learning opportunities through outside professional networks.

Collaboration Norms and Career Growth

Teachers' professional lives in innovative communities of practice depart radically from schools and departments with traditional or weak communities. The Oak Valley English teachers we quoted offer a glimpse of teachers' experiences of their jobs and careers in an innovative teaching culture. Such professional communities are collaborative and inclusive. Teachers take a collective stance on the issue of teaching expertise, seeing one another as resources for their improved practice with students in all of their classes. We use the term "teacher learning community" to define teachers' joint efforts to generate new knowledge of practice and their mutual support of each others' professional growth.

Oak Valley English department's program quality review captures the collegial spirit of such communities of practice.

In a schoolwide student survey, the English department rated higher than any other in students' eyes, as 74 percent described their current class as "excellent" or "good." . . .
While the above student outcome data indicate a strong English department comprised of dedicated and professional educators, the OVHS English staff still sees areas for improve-

ment and incorporates them in self-generated department goals. This and the fact that we continually share solutions and insights, actively pursue opportunities for professional growth, and care about the students with whom we learn, all make the Oak Valley High School English Department a great place to practice our art.

The policies and practices for assigning teachers to courses in teacher learning communities follow an equity logic: teachers who are least prepared in the subject should not be delegated to the most difficult classes, just as students weakest academically should not have teachers least prepared to teach in their subject. These communities acknowledge openly that classes with students who are least academically engaged are the most challenging for teachers. Oak Valley's English department chair praised their practice of rotating courses within the faculty: "I think our best teacher should be teaching those [skill level] classes, and it works out that way. It's very positive for the kids and for the teachers." He went on to say that teachers value this course assignment policy because "there isn't anybody who is sort of tracked into a dumping ground. Every year and a half, I'll be teaching 'Exploring Literature,' the same thing for everyone. That way, no one gets burned out." Such assignment practices engender inquiry into practice among teachers who "just kind of teamed up" to work on their teaching. The professional community becomes a locus of learning for teachers as they share experiences with the range of department courses and students. Teachers in such communities of practice find their jobs to be rewarding and professionally engaging.[7]

When teachers from the Oak Valley English and social studies departments told us how they feel about their jobs, it was hard to believe that they teach in the same school. Oak Valley English teachers of all pedagogical persuasions expressed pride in their department and pleasure in their workplace: "Not a day goes by that someone doesn't say how wonderful it is to work here," said one. In contrast, social studies teachers, weary of grappling alone with classroom tensions, reveal their bitterness and professional disinvestment. Several plan to leave the school or the profession. The chair hopes to secure a district administra-

tive position: "I need to change. I need to do something different. The kids have changed." The teacher in her department who
struggled to "teach concepts and analytical understanding,
rather than rely on didactic and objective information," feels unsupported in this fractured department, and hopes to land a job
in a local community college or leave education altogether. "I'm
ready to go, I'm ready to leave. I try, honestly, not to allow my
lack of interest in this job to, you know . . . [I try] to still be
good enough in the classroom."

Teachers' professional rewards and engagement differ substantially in these two Oak Valley departments.[8] Teachers in the
weak social studies department community describe their professional rewards and commitment as declining. In the collaborative English department, teachers experience their careers as
progressing—with professional growth and educational successes shared with colleagues. Clearly, teachers in both professional communities have experienced trends in their careers that
have nothing to do with changes in individual job status or mon-
etary reward, which social scientists regard as critical variables
for occupational success.

➤➤➤

Table 4.1 summarizes the distinctive patterns of teachers' professional relations and careers that characterize the high schools
and subject departments we studied. These patterns track with
differences in teaching practice and cultures highlighted in chapters 2 and 3.

A comparison of the two Mostaza district math departments
introduced in chapter 3 reveals contrasts in how teachers' work
lives and career experiences are organized in strong communities of practice that enforce traditions, on one hand, and that
innovate to engage nontraditional students, on the other hand.
Rancho's and Esperanza's math departments in the Mostaza
Unified School District organize their work in ways that engender qualitatively different professional relations and careers for
teachers—within the same district policy system, the same
teacher labor market, the same student population and community, and the same subject culture.

Table 4.1 Patterns of Teachers' Work Lives and Careers

Patterns of Teaching Careers	Dimensions of Teachers' Work Lives		
	Colleague relations	Assignment to courses and students	Professional rewards
Stagnant or declining careers (weak community)	Professional isolation; social relations enforce privacy norms	Seniority logic: prerogatives of tenure	Intrinsic rewards vary by students taught; esteem based in social standing of students and the profession
Divergent career trends (traditional community)	Coordination around course tracking and student testing	Expertise logic: teacher tracking by credentials	Intrinsic rewards vary by teaching credentials and assignments; prestige based in certified expertise
Shared career progress (teacher learning community)	Collaboration around teaching and learning	Equity logic: teacher rotation across course levels	Intrinsic rewards grow with collective success; pride based in professional growth

TEACHING CAREERS IN TWO MATH DEPARTMENTS

Math teachers in Esperanza and Rancho High Schools work in different professional worlds. Based on their relative expertise, Rancho math teachers are tracked into the department's class structure on the basis of their relative expertise and gauge their expectations for success accordingly. In Esperanza's math department, teachers rotate course assignments and work together to improve their practice with all students. Math teachers in Esperanza feel progress in their teaching careers, while many Rancho math teachers experience their careers as stagnant or declining.

Contrasts in these math teachers' work lives are captured by their survey ratings of collegial support for learning (figure 4.1 locates Mostaza math departments in relation to other public high school math departments in our sample).[9] The striking difference in teachers' learning opportunities between the two Mostaza math departments is especially significant in light of

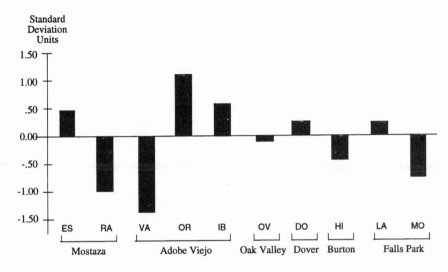

Figure 4.1 Math Department Differences in Teacher Learning Community

NOTE: Math departments are identified by school and district. Department scores are means of standardized teacher scores on the "teacher learning community" scale. The standardized scores were computed using the mean and standard deviation for all public school teachers.

their common embedded contexts. Not only do they share a discipline culture, but they also are subject to the same state mathematics frameworks, the same history of union-district strife, the same weak district leadership, the same desegregation mandate and rapid shift in student demographics, and the same problems of recruiting qualified mathematics teachers. Also, they have the same labor force characteristics, with only half the math teachers in each school having majored in mathematics. These departments have the least well prepared math faculties across all the schools in our sample of public schools, with the exception of the performing arts magnet school (Ibsen).[10] Differences in their professional norms and practices, and in teachers' work lives and sense of career, are socially constructed in nearly identical embedded contexts of teaching.

Teaching Assignment Practices

The career cultures of these two math departments in many ways mirror their classroom practices and beliefs about good teaching. Recall from chapter 3 that Rancho math teachers take pride in their rigorous testing, which regulates students' advancement through the program; holding students back is taken as a sign of the department's high academic standards. In contrast, Esperanza math teachers share the belief that all students can learn challenging math content, and the department has removed layers of remedial classes that nontraditional students would have had to pass through in order to enroll in introductory algebra.

Teachers in Rancho's math department rate one another, as well as their students, on their capacity to occupy places in the course hierarchy. Competence to teach higher-level courses is considered to be a matter of an individual's credentials in mathematics. As one teacher put it, "We have some teachers [who] are very strong in the department and capable. And then, I think, there are some who should go back for retraining so that we could have more teachers who could teach at the upper level. At the present condition of Rancho's labor force, few math teachers at Rancho are capable of rotating assignments which include high- and low-level courses easily."

Master schedule data corroborate our impression from interviews that Rancho math teachers tend to get "stuck" in their tracked curriculum. Of the fourteen teachers who taught in the math department from 1988 to 1991, only two ever taught math analysis or calculus and no teachers moved into teaching geometry, math analysis, calculus, or computer programming. Rancho's rigid assignment structure creates high dependence on particular faculty members, as well as enforcing a narrow conception of math competence and extreme teacher tracking. One year, with the departure of a high-track teacher, the department chair explained: "This year . . . I'm the only one able to teach precalculus." Another high-track math teacher in this school of fifteen hundred students remarked: "One year there were only two of us teaching Algebra 3/4, so that year I had quite a few students that I've had previous years, in Algebra 1/2. Now, I'm the only math analysis teacher this year, so—some of them got stuck with me for three years!"

In sum, career norms in Rancho's math department limit learning opportunities for teachers, as well as for students. The math faculty are specialized and tracked in their assignments and share low expectations for most of their colleagues. In this

faculty, there is no discussion of opportunities for collegial interaction, mentoring, or advancement to higher levels of math instruction. The strong department community enforces a hierarchical division of labor among teachers unequally prepared to
teach high school mathematics.

In contrast, Esperanza's math department acts on the belief
that students and teachers alike can advance through the math
curriculum. While Esperanza's math teachers are formally no
better qualified than their colleagues in Rancho, their progress
in teaching is supported by department colleagues. In this department, teachers are expected to hold high standards for all
of their colleagues, as well as for all of their students. They encourage one another to take risks, to try out new ideas and curricula. A veteran teacher commented: "I think I'm changing. It's
real time consuming . . . not something that you'd learn overnight . . . you fall on your nose a couple of times. And you'll have
to pick yourself up and try something different. I don't think you
can help but change with the population changing." Another
teacher said, "The faculty is very supportive of one another; we
all work together and we all have common goals."

The department is committed to developing the whole faculty's capacity to teach the highest level of secondary mathematics
instruction. One teacher explained the department's policy of
rotating teaching assignments:

> Special emphasis is given to rotating staff assignments
> amongst the various courses to foster staff development—so
> no one gets stuck. For example this has meant that over the
> years all staff have developed the ability to offer the calculus
> course. Consequently we are in a much better position than
> Longview H.S. where, when the calculus teacher retired re-
> cently, there was no one in the department to take over. . . .
> whereas we now have four calculus teachers.

Esperanza teachers talk about "growing" into courses. Regarding calculus, a teacher commented: "I grew into it last
[year]. . . . Another teacher grew into it the year before." Another teacher told us: "What we try to do is improve everyone,
so that eventually everyone will be able to teach it [calculus]."
Record data for the three-year period of our study confirm

teachers' reports about rotating course assignments in the department. In Esperanza, four math teachers (two with graduate degrees and two with B.S. degrees in mathematics) rotated teaching calculus. In contrast, among Rancho's four teachers with similar preparation in math (two graduate, two bachelor's degrees), only one taught calculus and another math analysis (precalculus). In Rancho's math department, teachers were stuck in their specialized positions within the tracked curriculum.[11]

Professional Rewards and Career Experiences

The Rancho and Esperanza math departments construct very different careers for teachers. In Rancho, teachers' chances of experiencing professional rewards and career progress depend upon their place in the department's hierarchy. High-track teachers have courses that engage their disciplinary interests, students committed to academic success, and respect from colleagues; their low-track colleagues teach content and students regarded by their colleagues and by the discipline more generally as marginal.

In contrast, Esperanza math teachers reap the rewards of professional growth and their department's success with all students. A veteran math teacher in Esperanza, who is regularly sought after for service on district and state committees, said that "what's really important [in terms of professional rewards] is what goes on in the classroom with kids." Rather than focusing on their formal expertise and status relative to colleagues, teachers in this department keep their eyes on student learning. Their collaboration enables them to realize the intrinsic rewards of succeeding in the classroom, and of supporting their colleagues' learning and success.

To support one another's learning opportunities, members of Esperanza's math department seek opportunities for professional development outside the school and bring back ideas and information to share with other department members. A number of the faculty have become leaders in the district: "Yvonne Albright and I have been real involved in the district curriculum, curriculum mentor teachers, me for seven years and Yvonne for five, so we have been involved in the changes. We report back what's happening and encourage our people to get involved."

Greenfield, for example, holds whole-faculty, four-day institutes before school starts each year, establishes mentoring relations for teachers new to the school, and holds mandatory faculty meetings at least bimonthly and "as they arise out of need." Prospect teachers hang out daily in a small faculty lounge, talking about their failures and successes in reaching their kids and exchanging advice and offers of assistance. They often team in the classroom so that they can try out group activities precluded by the standard ratio of thirty students to one adult. These occasions for communication enforce the norms of respecting all students and of collaboration and mutual support for teacher learning.

Ibsen. At Ibsen, both the performing arts program and the school's mission to promote all students' personal growth press academic teachers to rethink traditional standards of good teaching practice and careers. The school's mission challenges such common high school conditions as subject-centered practice, student tracking, and impersonal teacher-student relations. Ibsen poses particular challenges for traditional mathematics teachers, who are most likely to see their subject as static and student learning as sequential (recall the subject comparisons in chapter 3); performances that pull students out of classes virtually preclude traditional math instruction. Further, some math and science teachers are threatened by the dominance of performing arts in the school culture, which upsets the traditional status of their subjects and affords them less respect and deference than they would receive in a typical high school.

Up until two years before our study began, Ibsen was able to chose teachers for the school, ensuring that all teachers came willing to work in this unusual school culture. Since then, the math department has been a "revolving door" for teachers; both the school administrators and math teachers sent to Ibsen by the district express frustration with their shotgun marriages. Some math and science teachers experience their assignment to Ibsen as a downward career move, a loss of professional status and esteem. A teacher who taught a mix of math and science courses commented that being at Ibsen helped her to understand what the arts teachers feel like at a regular high school. She said she felt like "a one-eyed stepchild," merely tolerated in the school.

The collegial network and learning resources for this teacher community extend beyond the math department and even the school boundaries. Opportunities for professional growth are established through the web of social relations within and beyond the Esperanza math department.

Teachers experience their careers in Esperanza's math department as ongoing professional growth; in Rancho, many teachers feel that their teaching careers are stymied, and their professional rewards vary widely depending upon the academic track of their course assignments. Within the same district and community contexts, teachers of mathematics in these two departments inhabit different professional worlds.

TEACHING CAREERS IN SCHOOLWIDE LEARNING COMMUNITIES

Amid the high schools in our sample, we found three schoolwide learning communities—Prospect, Greenfield, and Ibsen High Schools. A look inside these communities provides further insight into workplace conditions that support high school teachers' professional growth and sense of career advancement. In each of these schools, teachers' professional lives are organized around the mission of academic success for nontraditional students. They stand out in relation to other schools in our sample on survey measures of teacher learning community (see figure 4.2, schools 14, 04, 08, respectively). Their professional cultures resemble those of the strong department learning communities of Oak Valley's English department and Esperanza's math department. Except for Greenfield, a private school, these schools are part of public school systems in large metropolitan areas of Michigan and California.

Greenfield's and Prospect's strong communities were forged through the schools' missions to work with students unsuccessful in traditional high schools. The fact that Greenfield is an independent school and Prospect is part of a public school system means that they have different capacities to attract and screen teachers committed to the school mission and culture; yet they are strikingly similar workplaces for both teachers and students. Ibsen, the performing arts magnet school in Adobe Viejo, grew into a strong collaborative culture through the leadership of its

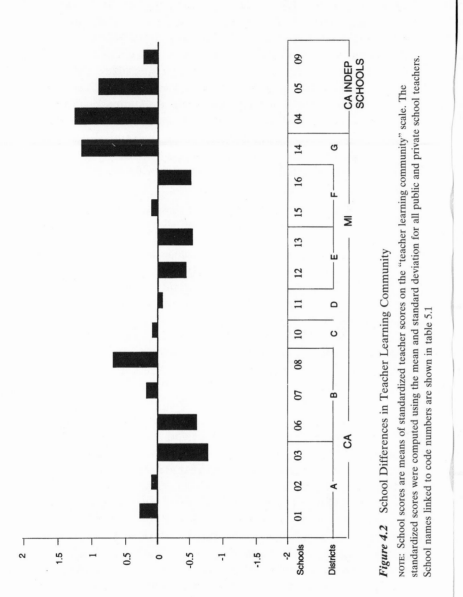

Figure 4.2 School Differences in Teacher Learning Community

NOTE: School scores are means of standardized teacher scores on the "teacher learning community" scale. The standardized scores were computed using the mean and standard deviation for all public and private school teachers. School names linked to code numbers are shown in table 5.1

founding principal and faculty, who continually challenge the boundaries and specialized cultures of academic subjects to engender and sustain schoolwide community.

Organizing Strong School Communities

Greenfield and Prospect. Greenfield and Prospect open each school year with intensive faculty orientations that reinforce the community's values, norms, and practices. The annual rite is essential to sustaining community, since about half of the teachers in each school are new to the school and to teaching. Teachers become committed or recommitted to working within these schools' structures for collective problem solving and learn how to participate as partners in constructing school success.

Without exception, teachers at both high schools talk about the enormous support they get from the school staff. At Greenfield, teachers said: "You feel like a team that is working together." "We learn over and over that the group is smarter than the individual." One teacher captured the spirit of Greenfield's community with a metaphor of keeping a boat going down the river when there are twenty oars and no one's ever been down the river before—the sense of charting a new course through mutual support and commitment. A Prospect teacher commented that "fellow workers are very important to make it through the day." Another offered: "I don't think any one of us would be able to survive in this job without the rest of the staff." The salient norms of these settings center upon valuing the students, who were rejected by colleagues elsewhere, and trusting the community as a vehicle for teaching success and professional growth. These principles challenge conventional norms of collegiality and notions of professional rewards, which highlight privacy and preferred assignments to high-achieving students. Further, teachers' commitment to the school community displaces the subject identities that organize work and relationships in typical high schools. Greenfield and Prospect teachers accept as "normal" class assignments that are outside their specialty and come to define their role as crafting content for their nontraditional students.

Staff community is nurtured by formal and informal structures that evolve to meet the needs of faculty and students.

In fact, we learned that Ibsen math and science teachers are held in low esteem by their colleagues in the district. An Onyx Ridge science teacher who had previously taught at Ibsen commented, while describing her career history: "There *are* no science teachers at Ibsen." Teachers throughout the Ibsen school community acknowledge the special plight of math and science teachers in the school, for whom being part of the faculty sacrifices rewards that derive from their subjects' privileged status in most schools.

Ibsen's principal and administrators are skilled in managing tensions between "real academic subject teaching" in secondary education and the school's mission and culture. They help teachers deal with the frustrations engendered by the strong performing arts program and achieve success without compromising school values. As one administrator described the school's approach to addressing the tensions:

> The way you do it is to find out how to make it work in both places. In other words, if you're a math teacher and you are having problems with Mary Jones who's the lead in the play, you can't come to me and say, "Well, we've got to kick her out of the play because she's failing my class." We've found that doesn't work. What we do is find a way for her to be a learning situation for both of us. And we've finally, I think, figured out how to do that with the math and science departments, who were undone trying to survive that.

By validating these academic teachers' plight in the school, Ibsen administrators are able to support their professional growth and commitment to inventing collective solutions to problems of practice. The principal told us that teachers developed a proposal to hire some of the "ringer" math and science students as helpers in a tutoring center, and the school added a qualified teacher to tutor students after school two days a week. She commented: "So some very good things have happened, based on what they saw as needs and how we could make that work for them. . . . They feel really good about it."

Collegial relations in Ibsen are a "whole school" phenomenon. Unlike their peers in typical high schools, Ibsen teachers interact regularly across discipline boundaries. The school's special mission and strong leadership support a sense of camaraderie that most teachers comment on and value. As one teacher noted: "There's more teaming here. It's the program." Even academic teachers get involved in Ibsen's major theater productions, working on stage props or costumes, for example, and teachers across the school seem to feel that they are "working together." Colleague relations at Ibsen go well beyond good team spirit. The school is a collaborative culture, and much of the energy of Ibsen's community comes from the staff's shared belief that "if we work together we can solve whatever problems we have." Both teachers and students learn and grow in Ibsen's strong problem-solving community.

Professional Growth and Collective Career Progress

The career values and rewards embraced by the Greenfield and Prospect teacher communities center on collective success in reaching students who otherwise would fall through cracks in the education system and society. Their jobs exact enormous energy from teachers, and the school community helps in any way to renew individuals' enthusiasm and sense of mission. A Greenfield biology teacher told us:

> I quit last year . . . when you are putting out that energy to carry them all the time, you need a return. You need something that fills up that loss. And you don't always get it. . . .
> I didn't have the energy to be as good as I could be. Once I had decided [to quit], I really felt at peace and then all of a sudden I got all this energy and they made some concessions in my time commitments and I recommitted for one more year.

In these high school settings, teachers often feel that the shared struggle sustains their personal commitment and effort. Also, they get real benefits from collaborating with colleagues on classroom practice, seeing this joint work translate into success with their students.

A story told by a middle-aged teacher after her first year at Prospect attests to the school community's power to redefine professional rewards and career progress. After telling us how she had been unhappy with her job assignment and actually afraid of the unconventional Prospect students when she was transferred there, tears came to her eyes as she told how proud she had felt when she recently ran into a group of her students in downtown Oneida and they hugged her right on the street. She had become comfortable and successful with her nontraditional students. She added that her husband, standing by as this tribute occurred, was appalled by their "jd" (juvenile delinquent) appearances and brashness. For this teacher, the moment was a precious professional reward, signaling advancement in her teaching career.

Like teachers at Greenfield and Prospect, Ibsen teachers derive professional rewards from their collaboration with colleagues and from their sense of collective success with students in the school. In the context of this school's emphasis on the performing arts, academic teachers find ways of working with their students that depart from traditional practice but that work and sustain their professional engagement.

The power of this school community to support teachers' professional growth and commitment to the school is illustrated by the experience of a veteran math teacher who came to Adobe Viejo from the Midwest because her husband's company had relocated him. The district assigned her to Ibsen, and she was just beginning her first year there when we first interviewed her. She was so angry and frustrated over conditions of teaching in the school that she apologized to us for becoming agitated and red in the face when she talked about her job. Among other comments about the school as a workplace, she said: "[The district] just put me here. Frankly, it's hard to get teachers to come here. . . . It's very kid-oriented and arts-oriented. It's hard on the arts teachers too. There's a lot more frustration built into this school than typical." During this interview, she also complained that the principal didn't back up teachers' authority with students, saying: "I want to close my door and have the administration deal with problems!"

Three years later, this teacher told us that her feelings about the school had changed entirely since that first interview. She said: "I now appreciate what we do for students here that doesn't happen in a regular school. I now see what the tradeoffs are between having a regular math department and this; the personal values and support are worth it." By this time she was an active member in the school community and a close colleague of the English teacher in the classroom next door. She acknowledged the professional costs of departing from the sequence and hierarchy of a "real" high school math department, but she also derived professional rewards from working with students who take an active role in their learning and with colleagues who support one another's professional growth.

Greenfield, Prospect, and Ibsen are notable for their collaborative cultures and for the professional rewards teachers derive from their shared work with nontraditional students. Professional engagement among teachers in each of these schools significantly exceeds the norm in typical public high schools.[12]

Teachers' experiences of professional reward and growth in these school settings is especially striking because they teach the kinds of students that their colleagues in typical high schools often give up on. They also teach in settings that offer least of the rewards that social scientists and policy systems emphasize: job status and salaries. Teachers in these schools experience professional growth because they work together to become better teachers and to become a better school.

HIGH SCHOOL TEACHING CAREERS

How high school teachers experience their careers depends a great deal upon the strength and character of their professional community. During the late 1990s in the schools we studied, formal career systems were minimal and inconsequential in teachers' professional lives; the sense of reward and progress offered by an incremental pay increase on the district salary scale was meager compared with the rewards of working successfully with a class of students. This is not to say that teaching salaries do not matter, because they do, but that salary increments are neither an incentive nor an adequate reward for the work of high school teaching. Incentives and rewards that matter most for teachers are the quality of their colleagues, of their course assignments, and of their students' learning. Possibilities for these professional rewards, and for rewarding teaching careers, are shaped in the day-to-day work lives of high school teachers.

Teachers' opportunities for professional growth and sense of career progress are tied up with the ways in which their school or subject department construes and organizes students' learning opportunities. In all of the high schools we studied, teachers and administrators believed that they were doing their best, yet how they organized their work differed in ways important for teachers' success and sense of professional accomplishment. In most high schools, teachers consider individual autonomy and seniority prerogatives as sensible principles for organizing their work together. In others, teachers work to uphold traditional standards for instruction by more closely coordinating their work to place students and teachers in levels of the curriculum. And in other high schools and departments, teachers try to give all students access to deep content knowledge by sharing courses and collaborating on instruction.

The careers that high school teachers experience—their sense of professional rewards over time—differ across these kinds of professional communities. In weak high school and department communities, particularly those in poor urban areas, teachers often feel that they are less successful in teaching than they used to be and attribute their career decline to changes in their students. Many burn out trying on their own to succeed, or they disengage from the job and profession. In strong traditional communities, teachers experience widely differing opportunities for professional rewards, depending on the academic success of students in the school or in the courses they teach; high-track teachers often experience considerable career progress at the same time as their low-track colleagues experience decline. In collaborative professional communities, teachers experience careers marked by collective accomplishments and a sense of continuing professional growth.

Teacher communities like Oak Valley's English department, Esperanza's math department, and Ibsen, Greenfield, and Prospect offer a vision of how rewarding high school teaching careers are constructed. In these professional communities, teachers see themselves as lifelong learners, share their expertise with colleagues, collaborate to improve their practice, and experience their professional rewards and career progress as collective.

Teacher learning communities break the rule of professional privacy that commonly keeps high school communities weak, and they resist myriad forces in secondary education to stratify students and teachers. Pressures on teachers to stratify students and sort them for highly unequal educational and economic futures come from the American cultural value of "meritocracy," the ideal of fair competition for rewards and opportunities, and from highly stratified postsecondary institutions. High school teachers' intermediate place in their subjects' hierarchies of certified expertise supports high school departments' tendencies to sort teachers into course tracks according to their credentials. Strong traditional communities of practice exaggerate these trends in typical American high schools.

The existence of teacher learning communities in American high schools, as well as their extraordinary success in nurturing successful careers for both teachers and students, frames the questions of how they develop. How do teachers forge understandings and ways of working together that run against the grain of American high school teaching, with what kinds of leadership, and with what policy supports?

CHAPTER 5

Teacher Communities in Embedded System Contexts

The variable character of high school professional communities permeates our descriptions of how teachers conduct their classroom practice and experience their teaching careers. On the one hand, all teacher communities play the same broad roles. They enact conceptions of practice and career and respond to "shocks" from the broader system (such as changes in student demographics, local economy, and public attitudes about education, policy shifts, and demands for new systems of accountability and assessment). They all manage in one way or another the press that institutional traditions and expectations bring toward particular conceptions of "good teaching," valid subject matter and knowledge, "good students," "good colleagues," and desirable teaching assignments and careers. Yet *how* teachers' communities construct such visions and play their roles varies substantially.

High school professional communities differ in strength and focus of mission, in locus and culture of practice—differences that matter profoundly for students and teachers alike. Most schools in our sample are weak professional communities for teachers, where classroom practice follows traditional teaching methods and where standards are lowered for low-track classes. Yet we found notable exceptions in schoolwide or subject department communities. Table 5.1 shows the distribution of our sample on key dimensions of professional community, noting also the particular subject departments that we analyzed as cases in this book. These classifications use survey measures of both collegiality and learning community—thus distinguishing traditional from innovative communities of practice. Our classifications also take into account qualitative differences in the *focus* of strong school communities, distinguishing mission schools from communities focused on teaching and learning. In particular, the college preparatory private schools and Oak Valley High School stand out as strong collegial communities in which teachers are united around a broad school mission but not around classroom practice. Similarly, Paloma's high standard for teachers' continued professional learning does not forge a learning community of practice across the faculty, as noted in chapter 3.

Although learning communities are relatively scarce in today's high schools, they constitute productive islands of professional practice important for the lessons they might offer reformers and educators. Their existence forces important questions, for example, What kinds of department and school leadership and resources support teacher reflection and collaboration to improve practice? What district and state policies nurture or discourage such communities of practice? We look into each of the embedded organization contexts of the teaching we observed for answers to such questions.

ORGANIZATION CONTEXTS OF TEACHING

We observed that the level of community that is closest to the classroom is the most salient for teachers, and thus most able to influence their practice and career experiences. A department may be a haven in an otherwise impersonal school setting; a school may be an island of professional support in a sea of district nastiness. Key to the nature of teachers' community in both instances is the character of its leadership.

The Power of Proximate Contexts: Subject Departments
Leslie Siskin (1994) calls departments "realms of knowledge" and sees them as the most important contexts for high school

Table 5.1 Types of Professional Communities in Teaching: Locating Our High School and Department Cases

	Strength and Character of Teacher Community[a]		
		Strong Community	
Culture of Practice[b]	Weak Community	Broad Mission	Focus on Teaching and Learning
Traditional	Rancho (03) Valley (06) Washington Academy (13) Monroe (16) Highlander (12) Dover (11) LaSalle (15) Esperanza (02) Scholastic (01)	*Collegial Community* Oak Valley (10) Juliet Wright (09)	*Traditional Community* Onyx Ridge (07) Rancho math department
Innovative		Paloma (05)	*Learning Community* Ibsen (08) Greenfield (04) Prospect (14) Esperanza math department Oak Valley English department

[a] Strong communities are defined as schools or departments with "teacher collegiality" scores ≥ .05 standard deviations above the national public school mean from the 1984 "High School and Beyond" teacher survey.
[b] Innovative cultures of practice are defined as strong school or department communities scoring ≥ .5 standard deviation above the sample mean on the "teacher learning community" scale.

teachers.[1] Researchers, Siskin observes, rarely acknowledge the differences between elementary and secondary levels, let alone the "invisible divisions"—that is, departments—within them. For example, at the time of her study, "department" was not even listed in the index of major studies of American high schools (1994, 10).

Nowhere is the power of department context and leadership more evident than in the contrasting communities of Oak Valley High School's English and social studies departments. English teachers experienced their department community as highly collaborative, innovative, and supportive of their professional growth; social studies teachers reported little exchange, support, or expectation for innovation and professional growth. English teachers had more space and time available for professional development than did their colleagues in the same school. Most telling, English teachers rated their learning opportunities more than one standard deviation higher on our questionnaire than did social studies colleagues down the hall.

These very different professional workplaces reveal how much department leadership and expectations shape teacher community. The English department chair actively maintained open department boundaries so that teachers would bring back knowledge resources from district and out-of-district professional activities to the community. English faculty attended state and national meetings, published regularly in professional journals, and used professional development days to visit classrooms in other schools. The chair gave priority for time to share each other's writing, discuss new projects, and just talk. The department created a space for faculty to eat lunch together by refurbishing a large storage closet, and thus became the only department with a common staff room. English department leadership extended and reinforced expectations and opportunities for teacher learning provided by the district and by the school, developing a rich repertoire of resources for the community to learn. Individual knowledge was a collective resource; even the much-maligned "one-shot workshop" added value to the department's storehouse of expertise since it was brought back, shared, and discussed.

None of this happened down the hall in the social studies department, where leadership enforced the norms of "privatism" and "conservatism" that Dan Lortie (1975) found to be central to schoolteaching. For example, the social studies chair saw department meetings as an irritating ritual rather than an opportunity: "I don't hold meetings once a week; I don't even necessarily have them once a month." Supports or incentives for learning were few in the social studies department. Taking a view that some members of her department were inferior social studies teachers, by virtue of their educational background or their commitment to coaching, she regularly put down or apologized for her colleagues in our presence. This department chair marginalized the weakest teachers in the department, rather than enabling or encouraging their professional growth.

Although they worked in the same rich district context and supportive school setting as their colleagues on the English faculty, social studies teachers encountered no learning community in their daily professional lives. Significantly, the only negative comments we heard about Oak Valley district as a place to work came from the social studies chair, who said, "Sometimes we feel like blue-collar workers. This district wants something for nothing with regard to curriculum development. The district talks excellence but doesn't want to pay for it. This is one of the few districts that doesn't pay for curriculum development." What other teachers saw as positive professional opportunity and respect for teachers' judgment—the responsibility to develop district curricula—she saw as professional exploitation. In mediating Oak Valley social studies teachers' relationships with their district, this chair negated the strong community and resources that the department faculty might have experienced.

These contrasts provide many insights about how teaching communities are sustained. They suggest, for one, that the social network Willard Waller (1932) saw as central to the world of teachers now applies at the department level in many high schools, rather than at the school level. They further show how department leadership can amplify or deflect learning opportunities in the school and district, and suggest the critical role of leaders as brokers and facilitators of resources for teachers' professional development. The coexistence of strong and weak learning communities within a single school also indicates that how resources are used matters as much to teachers' learning as does the availability of resources. Leadership in the English department created resources (such as time, space, and incentives to learn) and capitalized on those available in the district and the broader professional environment. Leadership in the social studies department failed to connect teachers to district and other professional development opportunities, and deflated teachers' interest in learning or change. These cases show the important ways that school leaders determine which conditions shape teachers' community and how those conditions in broader context affect perceived opportunity for professional growth.

Teacher survey data attest further to the importance of departments as settings for teachers to share and learn, and also to the role of department leaders in brokering resources to support such learning. We found that departments were just as important as schools in accounting for differences in teachers' experiences of support for their professional growth.[2] Further, teachers' reports of their department chair's leadership in obtaining resources was one of the factors that predicted strength of teachers' professional community.

School Communities: The Pivotal Role of Principals
High schools differ in their strength and character in significant part through the different ways in which principals construct their roles. For better of worse, principals set conditions for teacher community by the ways in which they manage school resources, relate to teachers and students, support or inhibit social interaction and leadership in the faculty, respond to the broader policy context, and bring resources into the school. The utter absence of principal leadership within Valley High School, for example, goes a long way in explaining the weak teacher community we found across departments in the school; conversely, strong leadership in Greenfield, Prospect, and Ibsen has been central to engendering and sustaining their schoolwide teacher learning communities.

Teachers' survey ratings of their principal's leadership show the wide variation in conditions that principals set for teacher community across high schools in our sample (see figure 5.1).[3] Principals with low scores generally are seen to provide little support or direction for teaching and learning in the school. Principals receiving high ratings are actively involved in the sorts of activities that nurture and sustain strong teacher community.

Standard Deviation Units

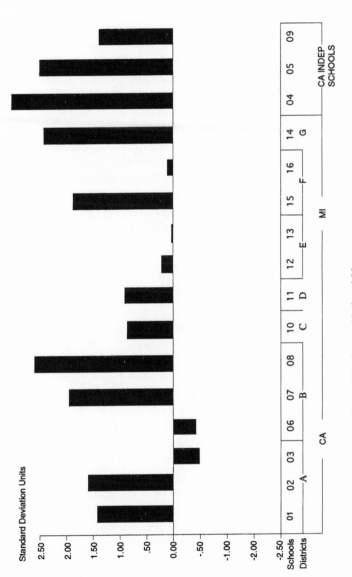

Figure 5.1 Principal Leadership in Relation to National Norms

NOTE: School means on the "principal leadership" scale are reported as standard deviation units above or below the national public school mean on the scale. National norms are based on the 1984 "High School and Beyond" teacher survey. The school means for our sample derive from the 1991 teacher survey. See Table 5.1 for school names linked to code numbers.

Differences in principal leadership across schools in our sample are only partly revealed by the numbers. Early on in our research, we noticed that principals who scored high on the leadership scale worked in qualitatively different ways with their school communities. When we did a "thought experiment," imagining how leaders effective in one school setting would function in another, it was immediately apparent that "effectiveness" was defined in terms particular to a setting, and that leaders were not interchangeable in their ability to stimulate and support a strong community of practice. For example, leadership for Prospect means working daily with teachers and students to validate and boost their sense of shared commitment to succeed in this school; leadership at Paloma means supporting teachers to participate in subject networks and academic events for students outside the school and sustaining parents' support. Principal leadership fits the school culture and context.

The significance of leadership becomes visible when a principal subscribes to goals or a leadership style that is incompatible with core values or routines in the teacher community. For example, a new school head brought to Juliet Wright from a traditional East Coast preparatory school lasted barely a year because his expectations about teachers' roles and their relationships with students were at odds with the established culture of this West Coast school. The Rancho math faculty completely ignored their new principal's mandate that the department change its testing policy and practice to expand students' opportunities to take algebra. We found that high school teacher communities, strong and weak, are robust in their resistance to attacks on shared values and knowledge built from experience. Fundamentally, leadership builds from trust and respect for the history and culture of a school or teacher community. The strong school leadership role played by Ibsen's principal in challenging new teachers' subject orthodoxies derived from the schools' values and traditions. Leadership to transform school culture builds upon its core values, rather than attacking them.

Principal leadership also spans school boundaries to mediate teachers' experience of broader system, community, and institutional contexts of teaching. Among the critical roles that public school principals play is managing the school's relations with the district, for better or worse. Differences in ways that Esperanza and Rancho principals responded to the poisonous Mostaza district culture and to changing conditions of teaching in their school reveal how differently principals can construct their role to either support or inhibit the strength and quality of teacher community.

Contrasting constructions of leadership. Esperanza's and Rancho's principals share similar challenges—tackling the issues of maintaining quality instruction following sudden changes in their schools' student demographics brought about by the district's desegregation plan, while simultaneously buffering the school from a stormy district environment. But the two principals see their jobs in strategically different ways, and so they have shaped qualitatively different school workplaces.

These principals face the same problem: How do you foster quality instruction in the face of new demands and student realities? Esperanza's principal sees the issue as a challenge for the school community, and has tried to strengthen the teacher community's ability to develop effective classroom responses. Rancho's principal locates the problem in the practices and attitudes of individual teachers, and so has focused on improving individual teacher effectiveness.

Esperanza's principal defines his role in terms of the school community and its capacity to change. "I see myself as the person who is ultimately responsible to see to it that everything that goes on at this school comes together in a way that's positive, and that the parent community, students, faculty, and staff work together to achieve our goals and objectives," he said. His vision for Esperanza underscores the connection of student success and faculty collaboration:

> We have a mind-set [here] that all kids can learn. That is our
> top priority—to teach students success—in the classroom,
> wherever students are active on campus. We are going to do
> what we can to help them be successful. And we are going
> about the planning and doing it in a collaborative manner. It
> was not going to be the decree from on high—"the principal
> says" kind of thing.

The principal's people-oriented leadership style focuses on persuading and bolstering, rather than commanding and controlling, faculty learning and change. He sees new forms of practice in his very experienced faculty as essential for Esperanza to respond effectively to the school's new students. "I think we have a very caring faculty," he said, "but also a faculty that's been around for a long time, that's really entrenched in the way things have been done before. . . . They need to change their teaching styles, because learning styles are so different, our clientele has changed so dramatically."

The principal calls himself the "head coach," supporting, pushing, and encouraging teachers to make change and their own learning a priority. Faculty members see him in those terms, too. "The new principal has worked very hard to offer us things that will help us do a good teaching job and help kids be successful," a longtime Esperanza math teacher told us. "He inherited a situation that was fairly stagnant. He has expectations for teachers, which I think we needed before. If you don't expect anything, you don't get anything."

The principal works to make the uncertainties associated with changed student needs, academic background, and social circumstances into occasions for faculty problem-solving and educational invention. To this end, he devised a number of cross-cutting, integrating strategies, such as committee structures, schoolwide planning groups, and annual faculty retreats, to create opportunities for ongoing discussion and, in the process, build a sense of community responsibility and engagement. He also initiated the Program Improvement Council, comprising students, teachers, parents, and community people, "to get input from all people and bring up issues from various constituencies . . . so everybody will feel they have someone speaking for them." These ad hoc communities have in fact enabled teachers to begin to assume collective responsibility for students' success, and to conclude that they all needed to make fundamental changes in their practices for the school to meet its goals. The vice principal told us: "Teachers now realize that they are going to have to change ways of presenting materials and strategies. One of the good old boys on the staff said one day to me 'maybe I'—emphasis on 'I'—'need to change.' Whoopee! Under this principal's leadership, teachers are allowed to grow, to have input on changes. . . . The attitude here is [that] now there is an opportunity to do great things, rather than [wallow in] the problems."

The faculty feel both challenged and supported by their professional setting. "Our principal has done everything possible to create a very positive environment at Esperanza for teachers and students," said an English teacher. "He wants people to be happy, he wants the students to do well. [He has created an atmosphere of] professional respect. Staff are highly regarded by each other and by the administration." At the time of our research, Esperanza's professional community was still coalescing. However, the norms and expectations the principal had established at the school level had enabled the math department to transform itself and be a model for the school—without the professional jealousies or backbiting sometimes seen when one academic department is regarded as somehow "better" than others.

Another important result of this principal's style is a dispersal of leadership. Throughout the school, teachers, staff, and even parents feel they have a voice and role to play in moving Esperanza toward its vision. Department chairs are charged with leading faculty to develop more effective practice for their new students. A district administrator credited this principal with "turning the school around" and added, "The district is proud of Esperanza. It was considered the drug capital of the district, with low academic standards, little self-esteem, poor ethos." To explain this transformation, he noted that Esperanza's principal is "just about the only principal in the district [who] meets regularly with department chairs."

Working with individuals. While Esperanza's principal approaches the problem of disappointing student performance as one of community norms and expertise, Rancho's principal focuses on individual teachers. He concentrates primarily on his "weaker" teachers, but sees his ability to "make a difference in their practice" hamstrung by factors beyond his control. He told us:

> My main role is to work with teachers to make them as productive as possible. And to make them feel good about coming to work everyday. Now the one problem with that is

there are some people who are happy naturally and they are
almost always the best teachers. The people who aren't very
happy in their own personal life aren't very effective . . . so I
can't deal with this part very well because that's private. . . .
Maybe they have the basic classroom management skills and
knowledge, but they just don't have much energy in what
they are doing. I find that to be true of my weaker teachers.

His strategy for motivating teachers involves one-to-one exchange: "It's simple. I do a lot of walk-throughs and acknowledge things that are going on that are really good. Little notices.
Also just verbally telling them. They like the typed notes better
than the handwritten. It looks like you are being more official.
And then the other part is, if you have a good idea, you come
to me, and if I've got to scrounge the money from somewhere,
if it's a good idea, I'll say, 'Well, let's do it. We'll figure out how
to get it done.' "

He frames his role in terms of individuals, despite his ac-
knowledgment of serious and debilitating problems at the school
community level: "You're going to hear more complaints than
before," he said. For one, he notes that Rancho teachers have
been heavily involved in the contentious union negotiations with
the district, and this anger spills over into the school and enforced "work to rule." But more important, Rancho's faculty
has been fragmented by the effective dissolution of their "unit
system," which divided the school into three houses as a way to
create smaller educational communities for both students and
faculty (see Siskin 1994 for details). The units themselves did
not function as coherent communities, and teachers lost their
departmental community as they were dispersed across units.
(The very cohesive science faculty was an exception; its teachers
literally picked up their desks and moved them back to their old
common departmental space.) The chair of the English department said, for example, "You lose the sense of the whole [now
that] . . . we work more in isolation from one another; I miss it"
(see Siskin 1994, 102).

The anomic and cynical character of Rancho's teacher community seems to poison teachers' attitudes about their careers
as well as about the school. In a sad comment on the sourness
of the school environment, one veteran English teacher, voted

"teacher of the year," noted in his acceptance speech: "My teaching is no longer outstanding. There is little motivation to be a good teacher, and no financial reward, no professional reward, no reward from society, and only on rare occasions intrinsic reward." The student newspaper further reported that "he [says he] enjoys his job for the isolation, the lack of administrative interference, and his ability to avoid contact with his colleagues" (Siskin 1994, 102).

Buffering teachers from the district. Esperanza's principal understands another powerful role for a strong teacher community: to provide an island of professional satisfaction. In fact, while he and his administrative team man the boundaries between the school and the district, mediating district toxicity as much as possible and securing additional resources as they can, Esperanza teachers do feel sheltered in a professionally enriching and satisfying community. Teachers clearly distinguish the significance of these two different professional contexts when they praise the principal for "giving people the opportunity to do the best job around" and simultaneously heap disdain on the district. "I would never recommend this district as a place to work to anyone," said a math teacher. "But I would recommend that they work for Esperanza." The Esperanza case shows that principals do have real power in terms of creating community, even within a district environment teachers experience as hostile and demeaning.

Rancho's principal also understands that school and district contexts comprise different professional communities:

> This school district has the lowest morale I have seen in thirty-two years. We're in trouble. We are losing young [teachers] because they are disenchanted. Pay is secondary to how they feel about their work. I have to keep reminding a couple of people here—just look at your own setting. Where do you come to work every day? How do you feel about where you come to work every day? Because you may move to another district and be in a school that's the craps. So, look at that first.

Yet he defines his role in ways that do not buffer the teacher community but instead expose it to the negativity of the broader professional context. He seems to feel that he has had little choice to do differently. Rancho's principal sees his own authority as having been emasculated by district administration, and himself as having little power to take the kinds of actions he thinks necessary to improve Rancho. He told us, "The other part of my role is to be the person who carries out the board's goals and objectives and the superintendent's wishes. Those aren't very clear, though, and you're not part of that decision-making process." District policy, in his view, is neither very clear nor consistent with schools' realities, yet it permeates the school. "The climate of the district really has an effect on schools," he said. "Every year there is some crisis in the district. Every year something new happens. It's either negotiations, [or] a wrong fit with the curriculum—current curriculum plans seem like a size 6 shoe on a size 11 foot."

District as Professional Community

As "local educational authorities," districts establish baseline conditions for teaching and teachers' careers. Districts hire, fire, evaluate, compensate, assign, and support teachers. Districts establish the professional contexts for teaching through the governance strategies they define, the professional development opportunities they provide, and the norms they establish for practice. The local school district also sits between state, federal, and national education policies and the schools.

As a focus for research and policy, the district has been almost as invisible as the department—despite its strategic position.[4] Yet we notice that districts themselves constitute a professional community that affects both teachers' (and principals') ideas about practice and their careers. In particular, while school-level interactions with students and colleagues determine teachers' professional rewards, their pride in their work and sense of professional value derive from their district's professional community. Districts also manage resources and set expectations that can support or frustrate teachers' school-level learning community. Teachers describe their district professional context in terms that range from "demeaning and demoralizing" to "supportive and respectful."

These differences show up in teachers' ratings of the three California districts as a place to work (see figure 5.2). Mostaza

Standard Deviation Units

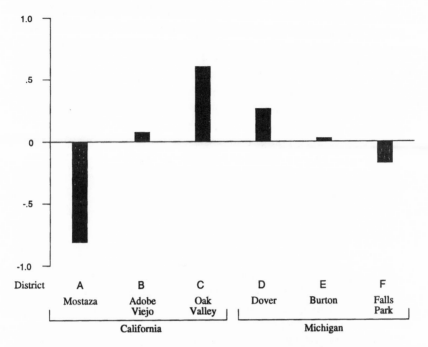

Figure 5.2 District Scores on the District Professionalism Scale

NOTE: District scores on the professionalism scale are teacher scores standardized using the mean and standard deviation for all public school teachers.

teachers' extraordinarily negative ratings of their district are no surprise given their comments that the district is "the worst in the state" as a professional setting. Teachers in Adobe Viejo see their district in a much more positive light, while Oak Valley teachers are enthusiastic about their district environment.[5] Teachers' assessments of their district as a community indicate qualitatively different experiences of the district as a workplace.

These different assessments of their districts find expression in the many ways teachers' describe themselves as professionals. Mostaza teachers speak with one voice in damning the district for its lack of respect for teachers. "You have to kind of bitch, almost get nasty to get the district to treat you in a normal way," observed an Esperanza social studies teacher. Teachers complain about the "insulting and demeaning" relations with "downtown" and characterize district staff as condescending: "The district always thinks of themselves as all-knowing parents," said a teacher. Teachers list the many ways that "downtown" has disregarded and excluded them from fundamental district-level discussions—for example, whether to designate their school as a magnet for a particular subject area or whether to assign it to teach a particular language or cultural minority.

Further, once these decisions were made, teachers claimed the "consequences were dumped on us." One said: "We received absolutely no preparation or help from the district. We were just expected to [implement the magnet program], even though we had no background or training"—more evidence, for Mostaza teachers, of the district view of teachers-as-interchangeable-parts. "You're told how you're going to run the schools . . . changes come from [downtown]," said a teacher. When asked on our survey if they were "proud to tell others than [they] work for this district," only 10 percent of Esperanza's teachers responded positively. Only 13 percent felt that Mostaza "inspires the very best in job performance of its teachers"; 34 percent said that district was a source of "considerable dissatisfaction" with their teaching job.

Mostaza's demoralized teachers approach new agreements with debilitating cynicism and work to rule; they tend to frame their work in terms of "job" rather than "career." A principal in one Mostaza high school, for example, told us that he was unable to find a teacher willing to take on the role of freshman advisor; teachers generally were unwilling to do anything beyond the activities absolutely required of them.

School administrators share teachers' negative assessments of the district, and even some of their imagery. Rancho's principal echoed the parent-child metaphor as he described the district context: "I have heard [principals say] often that we are looked upon by the district as naughty children, that we need to be reprimanded or put in our place or something. . . . We need to be treated like adults." Esperanza's vice principal described "downtown" as "just a mess," with strained resources and poor connections with the schools. She stressed the isolation school administrators felt: "The superintendent doesn't even have much of a connection to the high school principals. And [the principals are] where the power is. I don't know how he can be so politically 'inastute'—and I know that's not a word!" Esperanza's registrar echoed this frustration: "Our [school] administrators have no real control. It's a farce. Everything is controlled by the school board and the district."

In Mostaza, principals also talk of feeling professionally undermined and disregarded. Rancho's principal spoke of feeling emasculated and isolated. "There is hardly any opportunity to influence district decisions. To have a conversation [with a district administrator] I have to get on the phone personally and ask for an appointment," he said. "There is no support or understanding coming from downtown."

Mostaza administrators commented that inadequate structures or strategies for sharing information, confusion about responsibilities, and a general lack of trust block communication up and down the district. They noted that the district pays little attention to how it communicates with school sites. For example, staff at two Mostaza high schools were deeply offended to learn about the appointment of their new principals by way of a form letter from the district addressed "Dear Staff and Parents." The acting principal—who had worked hard to make changes in his school's effectiveness with their diverse student body and hoped for the appointment himself—was the most hurt and humiliated of all. He had no advance warning of the new appointments or the letter.

Principals also railed that the superintendent or district administrators have "no idea what the schools are about." They remembered the upbeat and supportive leadership of a former superintendent who, said the Esperanza principal, visited the schools daily: "He knew what was going on and what was wrong at each school. This [current] superintendent is never in the buildings." To this point, a district official commented on the lack of a coherent district community and saw the "invisibility" of district officials at the heart of the problem.

Teachers and administrators both decried the lack of clear, consistent direction from the district. Principals, especially, resent this ambiguity and uncertainty. The Rancho principal said, "If you have a superintendent and a board who are strong and clear about what they want then you can be a risk-taker and you are not in jeopardy." He also told us that "how the people downtown see you as a principal has a lot to do with how well you're able to carry out your [job]." The "naughty child" view in which he feels trapped has fundamentally eroded his sense of professional independence. "Autonomy doesn't mean being left alone," he said. "It means being understood and known. Autonomy means they trust me enough to try to improve in whatever areas I can." He feels that district-level constraints have stymied whatever steps he may have considered taking to strengthen Rancho's professional community.

The union's combative role in Mostaza reflects the district's history of disrespect for teachers as professionals. Although district administrators often point to the teachers' union to explain staff disloyalties and their contentious relations with teachers, evidence points in the other direction. Both a district administrator and a former superintendent agree that teachers in Mostaza are not always treated with respect. A former administrator told us that the "bad times and resentments [of this veteran teaching force] are reinforced every day." She recalled the dart board covered with a board member's photograph that went up in Rancho's faculty lounge after the board member "told a teacher that if she didn't like it here, go work someplace else." Teachers and administrators who seem able to negotiate the bonds of investment in the district retirement system in fact are looking for other jobs. "It's all unraveling," a former district official told us. "Every week I get calls from people—teachers, administrators, classified staff, district office people, every kind of employee— to tell me what's going on and to ask for letters of recommendation because they're looking for jobs elsewhere." This negative dynamic is integral to Mostaza's district culture, preserved by administrators' disdain for teacher leadership voiced through union channels and teachers' memories of their struggle for professional respect.

Teachers and administrators in Oak Valley, in stark contrast to their colleagues in Mostaza, praise their district as an exciting professional setting, one that expects much and provides much to support professional excellence. In fact, we heard the same phrase from the Oak Valley High School principal and from teachers in response to our question about what it was like to work in the district: "I feel like I have died and gone to heaven!" "I am so proud to tell people I work in Oak Valley." The union representative praised the district's commitment to high levels of professionalism: "The district is supportive and facilitative. It is a rather receptive district for new ideas." He was excited about the new model for nonadversarial relations his union was proposing because, among other things, "once more, Oak Valley's in the forefront."

Oak Valley teachers and administrators emphasize the many ways that the district supports their professionalism and supports school-level learning community. For one, district policies allow the schools a great deal of discretion in developing their own practices within a broad, teacher-developed curriculum framework. One teacher said, "Progressive thinking from a district allows schools to take on different shapes, different personalities. Excellence is key and the bottom line, so although it is decentralized in some ways, [in this sense] it is very centralized—commitment to excellence." An administrator who was new to the district echoed the same theme: "I am so impressed with all of the quality and the professionalism of the leadership in this district. The principals, the teachers . . . the superintendent makes his expectations clear—he wants excellence."

Another signal of professional respect is the district's support for teachers' learning and growth. From the annual kickoff banquet where teachers are introduced to the professional development resources available to them that year, to the fliers in teachers' mailboxes announcing events they may want to attend, to the brokering of grant and other monies for innovative projects, the district persistently seeks out and provides many opportunities for teachers to deepen their practice, experiment, and engage in professional exchange. The district frames staff development activities primarily in terms of a diverse "menu," developed by a committee of teachers, from which teachers can select activities that suit their particular classroom demands. Professional development in this district is planned by teachers and implemented by the district. Oak Valley provides good example of what "top-down support for bottom-up change" might mean in practice.

The Oak Valley district administrators vigorously seek outside grants and opportunities in the form of conferences, commissions, seminars, and the like. This openness to the larger professional environment attracts new resources and perspectives into the district, brings Oak Valley teachers into contact with practitioners around the state and nation, and gives teachers external benchmarks to assess their own practices as well as outside sources of professional acclaim.

Teachers' assessments of Adobe Viejo as a professional community are not as uniformly positive as are suburban Oak Valley's, but they nonetheless are remarkable given that it is one of the nation's largest urban school districts, with all of the attendant strains, demands, and diversity. Adobe Viejo and Mostaza are similar in terms of student and teacher demographics, together with the myriad pressures that challenge urban school districts today. Yet the district-level professional communities differ in many important ways. For one, while Mostaza's principals and teachers criticize their district's weak and inconsistent leadership with "no clear direction," as the Rancho principal put it, district administrators in Adobe Viejo work hard to convey district priorities clearly and to reinforce those priorities at many levels. In all our interviews with district staff, we were given the same benchmark for evaluating district policies and practices: How does it relate to teachers and kids? Both the superintendent and key members of his staff make themselves available to and communicate directly and often with parents, principals, school board members, and teachers. The superintendent regularly visits schools, meets with principals, and presents district goals, challenges, and accomplishments to the public.

The Adobe Viejo superintendent and his cabinet construct their roles with an eye to reinforcing and building district-level community. The district's restructuring plan, for example, includes all schools, if only symbolically. "It's important that no school feel left out," reasoned the superintendent. "We're trying not to do it like Dade [County, Florida], where a few schools participated in the effort and created an insider/outsider climate. I am trying to find a way to embrace the entire system, to include a range of schools and not to create a system within a system."[6]

Adobe Viejo district office personnel see themselves as "agents of change," as one administrator put it. "We are trying to move from being directors to being facilitators, to being supportive," said the superintendent. "Our goal is to support the work of principals and teachers," said an assistant superintendent. "We are here for them."

The superintendent acknowledges that district-union relationships are critical to the tenor of district-level professional community, and he acted quickly upon taking office to repair relations with the teachers' union in order to strengthen collective purpose and action at the district level. The major hurdle to district restructuring efforts, he said, "was a bad bargaining history with the teachers' organization. We now have a landmark contract that is compatible [with the superintendent's reform vision]." The superintendent credits this accomplishment to his collaboration with the union president and the fact that they "spent fifteen hours together, just getting to know each other."

Like district administrators in Oak Valley, Adobe Viejo district staff seek out resources for their teachers and administrators and take a prominent role in state and national professional settings. The district places a high priority on the professional development and engagement of its entire staff, from the superintendent on down to classified employees. For example, the superintendent created an Innovation and Change Leadership Group—composed of equal numbers of teachers and administrators—to focus on strategies for reform and professional development needs. When the group said it "needed to learn more," the superintendent told us, "I got money from [a foundation] to put together what I called 'Super Saturday.' I brought in Phil Schlechty, Marc Tucker, reformers from Rochester and Dade County, and other resources. Each school sent a team of five people—a teacher, parent, administrator, certified employee, and student. The charge was for the team to go back to their schools and talk with their colleagues about change." Similarly, workshops were held with his cabinet and the board "to educate them about what's going on in restructuring, to give them facilitation skills and other resources they would need to support the schools."

Adobe Viejo teachers have a clear sense of what their district "stands for." In our visits to district schools, we found that teachers knew their district's priorities and were able to discuss them. Everyone mentioned its emphasis on equity and meeting the needs of diverse district students; some complained that they felt pressured by this objective, but many took it for granted and talked about how they were addressing the district goal. Teachers agreed that high-quality opportunities were available for their professional development, although some expressed an interest in having a greater say about them. In short, while teachers and administrators have the usual array of complaints about pay scales, the program consequences of severe budget shortfalls, they generally see Adobe Viejo as a "good" district with a noble agenda and are proud to work there.

The broad dimensions of teachers' professional community at the school level—strength and focus of mission, collective or individual responsibility for teaching and learning, and conserving or innovative stance toward practice—also distinguish professional community at the district level in these three California districts. Oak Valley and Adobe Viejo are strong district communities. Shared norms, values, and expectations that support teacher innovation are communicated throughout the district. Mostaza, in contrast, is a weak district professional community, fractured by disputes, disrespect, and inconsistent leadership.[7]

Adobe Viejo and Oak Valley have a clearly expressed, coherent, and consistent district mission to enrich student learning opportunities. In Oak Valley, for example, it is apparent that district membership means something important to teachers about professional excellence. Teachers know that the district holds them to high standards of practice and their own learning. Mostaza, in contrast, lacks such clarity about district priorities, and leadership "flip-flops" in messages to principals and teachers about goals and expectations. Comments from teachers and administrators in these two districts underscore the importance of clear district goals and priorities to schools' sense of professional autonomy.

Teachers' appreciation of focused district leadership is reflected in their responses to survey questions regarding the influence of district policy on instructional content, their decisions about pedagogy, and their professional growth and development. Mostaza teachers rate their district much lower than do teachers in other districts. Without district leadership and clarity, principals and teachers feel they "can't take risks, exercise professional judgment," as one principal put it. The district's impact on teachers and teaching has little to do with hierarchical structure and controls and everything to do with the norms, expectations, and values that shape the district professional community.

Oak Valley and Adobe Viejo strive to create strong professional identity and community at the district level. These districts take teachers' professional development seriously, in terms of the expectations they communicate and the resources they provide. Mostaza teachers have no such support for their learning and growth, and they judge district resources to be weak and "in-service" opportunities to be poor.[8] (Professional mathematics associations and informal networks—not district resources—supported the remarkable learning and curriculum development we saw in Esperanza's mathematics department.)

Whither the State?

How do state policy systems shape the character of teachers' communities of practice?[9] Most apparent are state effects on the level of funding available to public education, especially in fiscally centralized states like California in the 1980s and 1990s. California's veteran teachers have expressed their outrage over the impact of the state budget squeezes and dwindling public support for education on resources available for classroom instruction and school facilities. California's Proposition 13 imposed a limit on the rate at which taxes could increase, and state government leadership did not provide new funds to ameliorate districts' financial hardships. At the time of our study, California was thirty-third among the states in total expenditures for education ($4746 per ADA [average daily attendance]); Michigan ranked tenth ($6268 per ADA).[10] These comparative differences had obvious effects on the schools: for example, Valley High School's business classes still had typewriters on the desks; shiny new computers were abundant in Michigan high schools' business and other classes.

Other differences between state education policies during the time of our study had a less tangible impact on teachers' workplace conditions, but nevertheless influenced teaching at the district, school, and department level. Starting in the mid-1980s, education reform policies and initiatives in California spurred a flurry of work on curriculum and talk about teaching standards, as we have seen in the California public high schools and subject departments in our sample. Michigan high schools were comparatively quiet during the same (1988–92) period. California's considerable investment in the development and implementation of new state frameworks for instruction provided curriculum, professional development resources, and instructional materials for teacher learning communities to use in working on their practice. In all of our California schools, teachers pointed to state frameworks as a spur for collaboration on curriculum and rethinking practices. State efforts to reform mathematics education have been substantial and sustained.

Most notably, the strong communities of practice we found during this era were located in the California policy environment—where new standards for teaching and learning were embodied in core subject frameworks, and where teacher professional development initiatives and subject-area networks were growing.[11] The state policy system and professional infrastructure were engaging challenges for practice and teacher learning posed by national subject area standards that emerged at the end of the 1980s. Teacher leadership in the Esperanza math department, for example, was growing in the context of state and district efforts to improve mathematics teaching and learning. Michigan teachers lacked similar stimulus or opportunities for learning at the time of our study. The only reference we heard in Michigan to resources for learning outside the district was from the principal of Prospect, the public alternative school, who pointed to important contributions the national networks of alternative schools had made to his own learning and knowledge resources for his faculty.

LEADERSHIP IN EMBEDDED TEACHING CONTEXTS

High school teachers' multilevel organizational contexts—department, school, district, and state—are not equally important in how their practice and career experiences evolve. The closer environments of school and department matter most. This is where teachers make sense of the broader contexts, where they may or may not forge shared values and commitments, where they do or do not find opportunity to learn from and with their colleagues.

Teacher surveys in the sixteen schools we studied corroborate our field-based observations that high school professional communities mediate effects of school, district, and state conditions on teaching practice and teachers' careers. When we analyzed survey measures of teachers' professional engagement and of their conceptions of teaching as nonroutine and subject matter as dynamic, we found that the "teacher learning community" scale was the only school context predictor. However, teacher learning community was predicted by measures of both principal leadership and the department chair's success in obtaining school resources; and they, in turn, were predicted by district professionalism.[12] The survey data are consistent with a view that principals and teacher leaders are pivotal in promoting or constraining the growth of teacher learning communities and in mediating conditions in broader contexts of teaching.

Embedded cases in our sample illustrate how conditions at different levels of the system interact in their effects on teaching. For example, the Oak Valley social studies department shows how weak department leadership essentially squelches the benefits of a supportive school and very strong district community. Esperanza illustrates how a strong school community can insulate teachers from a malignant district environment; and its math department further illustrates how department leadership can build upon school and state contexts, bypassing the district's problems.

Leadership for Teacher Learning Communities

The teacher learning communities we studied constitute unusual and valuable cases from which to learn about productive leadership for high school teaching. Qualitative and quantitative perspectives on the embedded contexts of teachers' practice and careers raise the question of leadership: How do school leaders manage and mediate the multiple contexts and pressures on high school teaching to promote such professional communities? How do leaders nurture communities in which teachers collaborate to invent practice that ensures all their students' learning and in which they experience professional growth and advance in their teaching career?

We encountered no instances to support the "great leader theory," charismatic people who create extraordinary contexts for teaching by virtue of their unique vision; nor did we see patterns in the strong leaders' characteristics—they were men and women with varied professional backgrounds. Some had been athletic coaches, such as Esperanza's principal; others had a strong discipline background, such as Oak Valley's English department chair. The female principal of Ibsen Performing Arts School came to high school from years of teaching in middle school, while Greenfield's male principal had a high school teaching background. Their leadership seemed to come from a strong commitment to making the school work for their students and building teachers' commitment and capacity to pursue this vision collectively.

Leadership for teacher learning community is situated in local contexts that frame challenges and opportunities for teachers' work. What are the particular resources and needs that students bring to the school? How can the teacher community build upon the student context, and what resources would support their success? How can site administrators and other school leaders bring community resources to support teaching and learning in the school and how can district resources and personnel support the school's agenda?

Leadership and teacher community are also interdependent. A strong principal affects the character and focus of teachers' professional community by collaborating with teacher leaders and respecting the teaching culture. Such principals empower and support teacher leadership to improve teaching practice. For example, Esperanza's math department builds upon the principal's vision of challenging instruction for all students; the faculty work to transform their practices to succeed in this vision. The principal cited the math department as an example of the kind of fundamental rethinking of practice he imagined teachers would need to do to succeed with their students. Oak Valley's new principal understood the primary role of departments in the school and was strengthening both the department chairs' autonomy and his communication with them. We saw one result of this move in the science department, which changed in one year from being a weak community of independent artisans to a strong community of collaborators attuned to each other and to the broad mission of the school. While our study did not focus on high school reforms and the problem of change, we consistently observed that leadership for change builds upon the strengths of the professional culture and challenges its weaknesses.

Strategies Leaders Use to Manage Embedded Contexts

Recruiting teachers. When asked about how they were or were not able to perform as leaders of their schools, all of the principals we interviewed mentioned first their ability to recruit teachers as key to their school's success. The idea of recruiting "good" teachers figured into each type of professional culture. In weak school communities, principals complained about the teachers they were assigned by the district; in strong traditional communities, leaders bragged about their success in bringing the most expert teachers to the school.

"Poor personnel selection can kill a school," said Onyx Ridge's energetic principal. "It takes a long time to turn around a school [through teacher turnover]. . . . The most important job a principal has is to select a good staff, because it is so hard to get rid of bad teachers." She said she is generally successful in getting the teachers she wants because teachers see Onyx Ridge as a desirable assignment, but more important:

> I manipulate and lie. I play games. If I said I want English teachers, the only ones I can get are top seniority and [I can't get interviews]. . . . To get around it, I post [the job] with an extended-day assignment. This allows interviews because it gives extra pay. . . . Plan B is that if the only teachers in the pool are turkeys, you can absorb a position, scheme, and interpret your staffing needs differently. My teachers support this manipulation [even though it is contrary to union guidelines] because everyone wants a strong colleague.

Leaders intent on building a strong school take active steps to mediate local labor force conditions. However, their conception of "good teachers" depends on both school context and the school's professional culture.

While leaders of traditional school cultures seek the most highly credentialed teachers, leaders of teacher learning communities look for teachers who are also strongly committed to equity in education and collaboration with colleagues. The headmaster of Greenfield, the private alternative high school, said hiring the right people is probably one of the most important aspects of his job. "I mean obviously we're looking for pedagogic substance . . . however, the way I do hiring is kind of different. . . . If it looks as though from a resume or a referral that a person will be interesting, I tell them about the school and watch their reaction. What I'm looking for are people who are really philosophers of education . . . people who think and grapple with the questions of motivation and engagement and growth and change."

The independent schools in our sample have more freedom to find good fits between their cultures and teachers' expertise and values. Recruitment as a community-building tool is unavailable to all, or even most, of the public school principals in our sample. Michigan schools struggle with the omnipresent threat of "pink-slipping," and teachers were uncertain days before the opening of school about whether they were sufficiently senior to retain their jobs. California's schools also wrestled with enrollment decline and fiscal crises that made it increasingly difficult to bring new faculty to a school. A Mostaza principal, for example, said how deeply disheartened and angry he was when "all the teachers I hired—every one—were dismissed in one fell swoop" as a result of district cost cutting.

In our public school sample, principals must work with strategies other than selection to build and sustain strong teacher communities—and they must work with their veteran faculty members. A number of common elements of leadership nurture professionally cohesive, collaborative communities of practice.

Establishing professional autonomy. Not all principals feel they have the support and professional discretion to act independently. Most Michigan principals, for example, define their roles essentially as managers, responsible for carrying out the rules and guidelines of their very centralized districts. However, our cases also suggest that a leader bent on nurturing strong school-level community will move to do that, despite district context. For example, while Rancho's principal sees autonomy as something bestowed or removed by district officials, Esperanza's principal sees it as something to be taken and assumed. He deals with shifting district mandates and requirements, while encouraging faculty to experiment, to change, to take charge of continually improving their practice.

Supporting teacher community and collaboration. Given this sense of professional footing, we see that leaders of the schools and departments where teacher community thrives make conditions of teachers' work together a top priority. They do not assume that teacher collaboration and invention are self-sustaining or that they can rely on isolated initiatives of individual teachers.

Leaders at all levels—department, school, and district—actively buffer teachers from outside disruptions and distractions. They tirelessly seek resources to support teachers' growth. While protecting their organizational boundaries, they also make teachers aware of the knowledge resources and opportunities for learning inside and outside school. Leaders keep windows open to new perspectives and ideas, acknowledging that the normative bonds of a strong community also can blind.

Leaders use a number of strategies and opportunities for teachers to work together in ways that clarify norms of practice and expectations for students. They create various structures to support conversation and exchange, both formal and informal, and enable teachers to negotiate different understandings about practice. At school and district levels, leaders use retreats, ad hoc assignments to cross-school committees or task forces, and other means to integrate views both vertically and horizontally within the system and to keep channels of communication open. They also understand the importance of informal communication; they ensure time and opportunities for it to occur.

Sharing leadership is a fundamental principle and dynamic of learning communities. Leaders spread responsibility and ownership for community values throughout the district, school, or department. For example, Esperanza's principal created new leadership when he gave substantive roles to department chairs and the various working groups established to tackle the school's instructional issues. Oak Valley's principal saw fostering and supporting strong department chairs as central to the success of his enormous high school. Adobe Viejo's superintendent charged a committee of parents, teachers, administrators, and community members with planning district goals. At all levels of a system, shared leadership becomes more leadership for professional communities.

Leaders at the school and district level use common work to focus teachers' learning and concentrate professional development resources. For example, Oak Valley teachers meet monthly to plan curricula guidelines and identify instructional materials for all Oak Valley schools. These district-level activities provide an ongoing spur and support to teachers and subject-area learning communities in the district. Esperanza's principal organizes all of the school's department, committee, and special project meetings around the topic of faculty response to the changed student body. This common work provides a point of convergence for teachers' inquiry—the joint enterprise for a community of practice.

Finally, leaders acknowledge that teachers' learning communities are not just professional, but extend to social relationships. We saw that attention to and celebration of events in teachers' personal lives—birthdays, family milestones—are important to the quality of relationships in teachers' communities as they are in classroom communities. Teachers in the strong learning communities of Greenfield, Prospect, Ibsen, Esperanza, and Oak Valley's English department value their personal relationships as a basis for reinventing their practice. Leadership sees the "social realities of school life"—which Willard Waller (1932) portrayed as the fabric of teaching but problematic for good practice—as conditions for sustained collaboration to improve practice.

The efforts and failure of LaSalle High School's principal to nurture an innovative teacher community illustrate how important such social relationships are to this form of professional community and practice. The principal's high leadership rating by teachers reflects his interest in reform and his efforts to provide teachers with knowledge resources (see figure 5.1, school 15). He gives a clear message to the faculty that they need to "change from their 1950s and 1960s teaching practices" in order to prepare their diverse student body "for 2010." He has established a professional development library and regularly brings ideas to faculty meetings or informal hallway conversations. He gives strong support to a cadre of new teachers "who are bringing new energy into the school," and he consistently tells veteran teachers, "You have to say to yourself, 'I have to be retrained, I need to find out new ideas.'" Yet he does little to stimulate conversation within or across departments or to provide a common focus for teachers' professional development. LaSalle's faculty community is fractured by its heavily tracked curriculum ("It's like two schools," said a science teacher), by the uncertainties associated with annual pink-slipping, and by peculiar space arrangements that disperse members of a department across the huge building. These instructional, bureaucratic, and administrative choices result in little collegial contact. As one teacher put it, "We're like ships passing in the night." In contrast, leadership for teacher learning community builds broad social networks as vehicles for learning and invention.

▼▼▼

The existence and success of teacher learning communities in American high schools raises questions of how such environments for teaching might be promoted and sustained in the policy environments of secondary education. What challenges do weak high school communities and strong traditional communities of practice pose for change? What conditions in the K–12 policy system and broader contexts of high school teaching promote or inhibit the development of teacher learning communities? What policy strategies underway at the turn of the century support this vision of professional practice? Chapter 6 addresses these questions about the future of teaching in American high schools.

CHAPTER 6

High School Teaching
in the Twenty-first Century

When Dan Lortie contemplated the future of teaching a quarter century ago, he envisioned an ideal very much like the learning communities of teachers we found in some of the high schools and subject departments we studied. Teacher inquiry and collaboration to build shared knowledge, he argued, would be essential for the profession's claim to authority and autonomy from growing school bureaucracies. But he foresaw deep-seated resistance to such change in the culture of teaching:

> [T]he ethos of the occupation is tilted against engagement in pedagogical inquiry. *Reflexive conservatism* implicitly denies the significance of technical knowledge, assuming that energies should be centered on realizing conventional goals in known ways. *Individualism* leads to distrust of the concept of shared knowledge; it portrays teaching as the expression of individual personality. *Presentism* orientations retard making current sacrifices for later gains; inquiry rests on the opposite value. (1975, 240; emphasis added)

The learning communities we describe in earlier chapters of this book offer a concrete vision of the profession's potential to change its culture in response to twenty-first-century challenges to American education. Yet prospects for widespread change in the ethos of high school teaching depend on conditions in the broader cultural and policy contexts of secondary education, as well as on the professional commitments and initiative of teachers and school administrators.

RECULTURING HIGH SCHOOL TEACHING

Building learning community into the work lives of American high school teachers is fundamentally a problem of reculturing the profession—changing the ethos of teaching from individualism to collaboration, from conservatism to innovation. Teachers will need to question widely held values and beliefs about desirable high school teaching jobs and good teaching practice. Efforts to change teaching by restructuring schools or by mandating new education standards will fail if teachers lack the vision and will to change their professional lives and practice.[1]

Teachers' considerable professional agency notwithstanding, traditions in education and society can shape their values, beliefs, and feelings about teaching, students, subject, colleagues, and careers. Secondary school teachers navigate an especially complicated cultural terrain. Because high schools occupy a strategic, intermediate position in the education system, teachers negotiate values and traditions of teaching in elementary grades and in higher education. For example, high school teachers manage tensions between learner-centered and subject-centered teaching cultures and between the school and the discipline as professional home. Further, as gatekeepers of students' access to higher education, high school teachers are subject to expectations and pressures from parents, colleges and universities, and the public about how to prepare and allocate students into an extremely stratified higher education arena.[2]

The prospects and challenges for developing innovative communities of practice in high schools thus implicate the cultural contexts of American secondary education. The currency of particular values and standards for high school teaching influences the ways in which teachers think about their work—and so can inhibit or promote change within the culture of high school teaching.[3] The support or lack of support that teachers find for particular principles of teaching within their school and professional circles, among friends, and in the media—as well as in their policy system—largely determines whether they will pursue them in practice. At the turn of the century, we see cultural trends that alternately encourage and discourage a vision of teacher learning community for the profession.

Changing Norms of Professional Relations:
From Individualism to Collaboration

The primacy that teachers historically have placed on autonomy and privacy reflects broader cultural notions of how professionals practice.[4] Traditionally, an occupation is granted "profession" status on the basis of its practitioners' expertise and ability to exercise sound and independent professional judgment. Private practice has been the prototype of professionals' work and the basis for their esteem. This view of professional practice encourages an understanding of expertise as an individual attribute and discourages professional sharing and collaboration. Just as standards of "real school" shape the organization and routines of schools (Metz 1990b), cultural notions of "real profession" influence how teachers conduct their work lives and experience their career.

Nonetheless, over the century, the work of professionals has generally become more organized and collaborative (Scott 1992, 253–56). We conjecture that new principles and models of professional practice have been finding their way into the culture of teaching. Teachers may well question privacy norms for teaching in light of news articles on discoveries by teams of scientists, popular writings about collaborative norms of business organizations, conversations with family and friends about their work lives, and inspirational speeches at professional development events.[5] High school teachers also are likely to pick up on changing work norms in the environments of the disciplines they teach. At the turn of this century, the notion of cultural inertia and resistance to collaboration seems less viable as an account of privacy's persistence in teaching.

An issue fundamental to the future of teacher learning communities in high schools concerns the locus and nature of joint enterprises that they might develop. Ideals of collaborative organization culture and team productivity in the broader culture make no sense when the curriculum of teaching is parceled out and bounded by classrooms. Anthropological research on adult learning in "communities of practice" (Lave and Wenger 1991; Wenger 1998) identifies key elements and dynamics of professional learning communities and helps to define challenges for framing the work of teacher communities. Such communities are characterized by mutual engagement, joint enterprise, and shared repertoires of practice (such as materials and concepts). This literature from outside education raises a key issue for the future of high school teaching: around what problems of practice will teachers share their work and build community?

The discipline identities and subject subcultures of high school teaching are critical contexts for defining shared work and building communities of practice. Leslie Siskin discusses at length in her book *Realms of Knowledge* (1994) the distinctive languages, perspectives on teaching and students, professional reference groups, and social networks that frame subject subcultures in high schools. School systems enforce these boundaries of subject cultures through state credentialing systems, district hiring practices and contracts, and high schools' typical departmental structure. Subject-based professional identities also find expression and encouragement in the disciplinary boundaries of knowledge and work in typical American colleges and universities.

High school teachers' identities and contractual responsibilities as subject educators define potential for strong department-based communities of practice, but they constrain teachers' mutual engagement at the school level. Indeed, researchers whose work focuses on schools as social organizations sometimes argue that high school subject departments "fragment" school organization and undermine the development of high school community.[6] Schoolwide communities of practice that we as well as other researchers have found are on the margins of secondary education, in small high schools with a mission—defined by a special program or special student needs—that forges joint enterprise across the school's faculty.

Absent mutual engagement in shared goals and common work, teachers are likely to experience pressures and structures designed to build schoolwide community as "contrived collegiality," to use Andy Hargreaves's (1991) term. While overlapping communities of practice might develop at department and school levels around different kinds of work to support student learning and engagement, subject departments are likely to remain important contexts for teacher community in comprehensive high schools. Leadership to build schoolwide community would bring teachers together around challenges and responsibilities that go beyond a subject faculty's shared responsibilities for teaching and learning in their discipline.

A further critical issue concerns the cultures of teaching that high school communities of practice develop. The fact that some strong high school communities in our study enforced teaching routines and failed large proportions of students was unanticipated by prior research on school community and was also contrary to state and national education policy goals. What messages about good teaching in the broader institutional environment of American secondary education might shape the discourse and enterprise of high school teacher communities?

Changing Norms of Teaching Practice:
From Reflexive Conservatism to Innovation

Teacher learning communities' innovations threaten traditions of pedagogy, content, and student outcomes in American high schools that the public generally takes for granted as good education practice. Teaching innovations in high school classes and departments are not culturally neutral. The currency of, and politics surrounding, beliefs and ideas about effective educational practice will likely shape the future of high school teacher communities.

Traditional education practice—characterized by reliance on textbooks for content and memorized facts and skills as learning outcomes—remains the norm in American high school classrooms. Evidence is mixed regarding public demand for this form of instruction versus the innovative, student-centered practices that we observed in the classrooms of teachers who were members of learning communities. While the business community calls repeatedly for more emphasis on students' problem-solving skills and flexible reasoning in content domains (SCANS 1992), public reaction to state or local standards promoting such outcomes has been quite negative in some places. For instance, in the late 1990s, efforts to gear mathematics education toward strengthening students' mathematical literacy, over more traditional forms of math learning, encountered organized resistance in states such as California and Massachusetts.[7] Pressures on teachers in some states or districts to adhere to traditional routines of teaching surely discourage them from joining together in communities to revise their classroom practice.

At the same time, research evidence overwhelmingly challenges the efficacy of teaching conventions found in most American high schools. The National Research Council's (NRC) report *How People Learn* (Bransford, Brown, and Cocking 1999) integrates research findings across disciplines to identify principles and conditions of effective learning environments. This national panel of scientists details a vision of teaching that radically departs from traditional practice—calling for learning environments that are student centered, knowledge centered, assessment centered, and community centered. Further, widely publicized results of the Third International Mathematics and Science Survey (Schmidt, McKnight, and Raizen 1996) press for reform of high school mathematics and science teaching. The assessment finds that the weak performance of U.S high school students correlates with their teachers' extraordinary emphasis on topical coverage or breadth, as opposed to depth, in mathematics and science instruction. The TIMSS findings and conclusions dovetail with urgings from the NRC report for rethinking instruction in U.S. high schools.

At the same time, secondary education currently is subject to increasing state and district accountability centered on student performance on standardized tests. In most cases, the tests tap basic skills and factual knowledge and thus can inhibit teachers' work to build students' deeper understandings and flexible reasoning in subjects, especially in schools serving poor and academically weak students. Schools and teachers sanctioned on the basis of aggregate test scores are drilling their students to pass the tests, even when they believe that the learning is of limited enduring value and the practice is educationally unsound.

Teachers in American high schools grapple with two competing cultural and policy mandates for the future of their practice: to enforce traditional curriculum and assessment standards that emphasizes basic skills and scores on norm-referenced tests or to innovate to create opportunities for all students to achieve standards of higher-order content knowledge and problem solving.[8]

Further constraints on innovation stem from American secondary education's original mission: to sort students for different futures, as well as to educate them. The cultural ideal of "meritocracy" makes it desirable and fair for high schools to establish unequal educational opportunities for students, as long as screening and placement criteria are objective. Curriculum tracking and emphasis on standardized testing in secondary education reflect a logic of fair competition. These values and practices significantly inhibit education reform in high schools. National education standards to enhance equity and reform efforts to detrack secondary school programs have met considerable political resistance within and outside education.

Educators, analysts, and constituents alike divide in their views on structured inequality in American comprehensive high schools. Disagreements center on definitions of educational equity and technical versus normative standards for organizing and assessing students' learning opportunities.[9] How schools and teacher communities address tensions between the socializing and sorting goals for secondary education is among the most practically important and intellectually fascinating problems of high school teaching.[10]

❧❧❧

The divergent professional cultures of high schools and subject departments that we found during the 1990s express cultural discontinuities in American education that frame fundamental, if invisible, problems for teachers' work. Considerations of policy strategies to improve the prospects for teacher learning community would keep in the fore inhibitions of traditional teaching culture and broader cultural tensions surrounding secondary education.

POLICY STRATEGIES TO BUILD
TEACHER LEARNING COMMUNITIES

Chorus and refrain in our study of teaching and our understanding of the conditions that support teachers' learning and change is the critical importance of professional discourse and inquiry. Opportunities for teachers to talk with colleagues about teaching, consider new ways of doing things, and hammer out shared understandings about goals were common across diverse environments where practices were rethought in ways that benefited both teachers and students. Teachers' ability to respond effectively to the diverse needs, interests, and talents students bring to their classrooms and to implement principles of teaching that motivate reform will depend upon their ability to have these relationships.

During the 1990s, there were signs that the policy system was shifting its theoretical base, from rational coordination, contracts, and other aspects of bureaucratic organization that have structured the grammar of schooling for the past century, to professional relationships and ties. For example, policy makers at all levels of government have turned to practitioner networks and communities as strategies for generating and sharing knowledge about practice and implementing new curricula frameworks.[11] However, this new relational or social systems approach to improving teaching is limited in its capacity to nurture the learning communities we portray here.[12] As we discovered, not all strong teacher communities develop knowledge to improve their collective success with students. Policy to support such communities thus must go beyond providing opportunities for social interaction to engage cultures of practice. The challenge for policy and practice posed by the vision of teacher learning communities is to engender norms of inquiry, innovation, and shared accountability to support effective teaching practice and rewarding careers.

Building Communities of Practice into Teaching Careers
As large proportions of today's teachers move into retirement, new teacher induction is an important opportunity for policy and leadership to reculture high school teaching. Experiences of beginning teachers are pivotal to the profession's future. Will new teachers be left to sink or swim in the anomic environment of weak school communities or in the low-track classes of traditional academic departments; or will they enter teacher communities that practice together to improve their teaching? What norms of practice will senior colleagues convey? Will beginning teachers find professionalism in their high schools and a sense of pride in the profession?

Policies to reform teacher education would seek to prepare teachers for collaboration with colleagues as a normal part of teaching practice, challenging conventions of teacher education that inhibit cooperation. A quarter century ago, Dan Lortie lamented traditions in higher education that work against a vision of inquiring teacher communities: "Conventional coursework in education, as in the arts and sciences generally, underscores individualistic modes of work in a zero-sum competitive race for grades; modifying such arrangements to include sharing of tasks and rewards could prepare teachers-to-be for closer working relationships" (1975, 237).

New national standards for teacher education call for teacher research applied to real problems of practice, which could engender expectations and experience conducive to inquiry in professional communities (National Commission on Teaching and America's Future 1997). The standards aim to establish community for beginning teachers and to nurture teacher leadership through extended clinical experience and school-university relationships.[13] Such approaches to new teacher socialization are promising vehicles for reculturing teaching toward innovative communities of practice.

Policy focused on placing teachers in jobs for which they are well prepared seems an obvious strategy to ensure teachers' capacity to contribute to their students' and colleagues' learning. Yet this condition frequently is unmet in poor urban districts and schools, where classrooms are often staffed with teaching novices. Just when standards for education in the disciplines call upon deeper subject and pedagogical knowledge among teachers, economic and population trends have created highly uneven demand for teachers across regions of the country. Inequalities in the desirability of teaching jobs exacerbate the problem, in that the most qualified teachers are attracted to the most favorable professional environments, often in districts serving relatively affluent communities. Teacher labor force conditions set constraints and opportunities for teacher assignment policies and practices. In turn, they shape potential for innovative communities of practice to grow in the teaching profession.

Although our data do not bear directly on this issue, it seems likely that some critical mass of teachers experienced and well-grounded in their subject discipline is essential for teacher learning communities to grow and prosper. Research on learning in student communities highlights the role of "distributed expertise" in generating new knowledge (Brown and Campione 1990, 1994, 1996). Considerations of teachers' capacity to contribute to, and learn from, communities of practice might prompt local school systems to assign teachers to ensure a mix of subject preparation and teaching experience in schools and departments. Challenging the job hierarchies of informal career systems within large school districts will be critical to establishing teacher learning communities across U.S. high schools.

Another prong of policy to promote teacher learning communities is to reculture careers in teaching. Strategies would aim to define professional rewards and status in terms of teachers' ongoing professional growth and contributions to knowledge of practice. A conception of the teaching career as embedded in practice opposes the competitive hierarchical career systems that some see as key to professionalizing teaching. Incentive systems to build the kind of career progress that learning community engenders would expand teaching jobs to include mentoring colleagues and participating in networks beyond the school. They would legitimize and reward the inventions and professional accomplishments of teacher communities of practice.

National and state credentialing systems have moved in this direction and promise to broaden standards for teaching excellence to include collegial collaboration to improve practice. Most prominent in this movement is the National Board for Professional Teaching Standards (NBPTS) certification system established in the late 1990s to assess and certify excellence in teaching among veteran teachers.[14] The NBPTS assessment standards call for evidence of a teacher's successful work with colleagues, as well as evidence of effective classroom practice. The board thus establishes professional standards for teaching practice that extend to teachers' participation and leadership in professional community.[15]

The state complement to this initiative, the Interstate New Teacher Assessment and Support Consortium (INTASC), currently involves more than thirty states in developing beginning teacher assessments and supports designed to prepare teachers ultimately for board certification. The state credentialing standards developed in conjunction with the national initiative could further instantiate a norm of collaboration for the profession and help to build leadership within the policy system for learning community as a vision of the profession's future.

Extending Teacher Communities' Knowledge Resources
A growing number of states and their districts have developed education standards such as those embodied in the California subject frameworks at the time of our study. The state standards movement embraces principles for teaching in core high school subjects that national subject associations have developed over the past decade, beginning with the 1989 publication of curriculum standards by the National Council of the Teachers of Mathematics. They highlight goals for student learning considered by many educators and business leaders to be basic skills for the twenty-first century: understanding a discipline's terrain, knowing how to use discipline knowledge and skills to solve complex real-world problems, and learning to seek new knowledge to solve problems and advance one's skills. Further, they aim for greater educational equity and success with diverse learners by making learning outcomes clear and ensuring multiple or cyclical entry points for students to engage core discipline concepts and develop deep content knowledge.

The underlying principles of these standards build on scientific discoveries in cognitive science about the nature of learning and call for significant change from the traditional conventions of teaching. The standards go to the core of the "triangle" of instruction, calling upon teachers not only to assess their students' prior understandings and guide their learning into new reaches of content knowledge and skills but to establish classroom environments in which students can learn as members of communities.[16] They challenge teacher-dominated, transmission-oriented traditions in American secondary education that emphasize sequential and superficial coverage of many topics.

New teaching standards thus present significant challenges for teacher learning and professional development across American schools. Learning demands on teachers include "unlearning" habits of mind and practice in education and learning to invent ways of bringing students more deeply into a discipline (Ball 1993). At the same time, the standards present opportunities for professional development. Professional, state, and local standards documents and the teacher resources that go along with them provide a means for communities of practice to innovate and improve their teaching.

Policy strategies to build knowledge resources thus depart from traditional "teacher training" to invest in intensive, sustained professional development institutes and on-site coaching. At the same time, these strategies promote teachers' participation in professional associations and networks to support ongoing exchange between high school professional communities and their subject colleagues. In general, conditions in American education today fall abysmally short in this regard. National survey data for 1993–94 show that although about half of all teachers had some professional development during the year, only 15 percent spent nine or more hours in any area of professional development. However, rates of teacher participation in longer-term professional development are higher for states that have invested in professional development as a strategy to improve instruction.[17]

Principles for professional development policy, practice, and initiative that come from nearly two decades of U.S. education reform underscore our conclusion that teacher learning communities constitute the best context for professional growth and change. Reformers of various stripes conclude that effective professional development has a strong site-based component, enables teachers to consider their practice in light of evidence and research, and is grounded not only in knowledge of teaching, but in relation to specific students and specific subject matter.[18] If these principles become the basis for serious reform in professional development programs supported by states and districts throughout the country, they could significantly enhance both teacher learning and opportunities for learning communities to grow.

Investing in teachers' learning community as a strategy to build teachers' capacity for effective teaching in twenty-first-century classrooms entails a shift from system policies that seek to prescribe standardized practices to those that aim to strengthen teachers' judgment and opportunity to learn. Policy strategies would promote teachers' engagement in learning outside, as well as inside, the education system—in professional associations, teacher unions, subject matter networks, informal professional development groups. States and districts are ill equipped to develop or provide these knowledge resources, and teachers' professional organizations can contribute critical expertise to government-sponsored investments in teachers' learning and change. Similarly, a partnership of government and professional initiatives can result in more powerful and coherent resources for teachers' learning and community. Yet, with a few important exceptions, government and profession still generally operate in separate spheres and come together more often as contenders than as collaborators.

Reforming the School Policy System

Our research highlights potential for change at the "bottom" of the education policy system and for building knowledge resources from outside the system. However, we expect that the animated, inquiring communities of teaching that we describe here will remain exceptional in American high schools without deliberate change at the "top" of the policy system—that is, the local, state, and federal policy contexts outside the school.

Teacher learning communities are thwarted and derailed by more than the profession's traditional ethos and institutional cultures of education; they also are constrained by the structures and mandates that make up the regulatory frameworks and policy contexts within which teachers teach. For example, California teachers' efforts to collaborate on standards and assessments for their high school students were thwarted by state policy that reduced their time for professional development by more than half in 1999–2000. District teacher evaluation policies often foster competition and privacy rather than collective work. Teachers energized by collaborative work at their schools complain bitterly about district requirements that they attend workshops irrelevant to them, using up scarce professional development days. Teachers motivated to inquire into the achievement of their students as they wrestle with issues of equity and high standards for all students often find themselves stalled by district practice that precludes disaggregating data in the way they need.

Policy makers have become aware of the uncertain and

often unpredictable relations between policy and practice, but the policy response remains incomplete. In reaction to research showing that educators working at the bottom of the system—the street-level bureaucrats, as Weatherley and Lipsky (1977) dubbed them—needed to adapt new information and reform initiatives to fit their own realities, policy makers launched strategies to provide "top down support for bottom up change" (see, for example, McLaughlin 1987). Yet these policy supports often fall short because they operate within and through unchanged policy structures—licensing and certification or accountability structures, for example—and do not represent change at the top.

Yet change at the top that is based in considerations of policy coherence and fit with a culture of teacher learning and inquiry seems essential to teachers' effective use of new resources like subject area networks. More likely than not, this fit is missing. For example, some states and districts simultaneously support student-centered standards of teacher practice found in the National Board of Professional Teaching Standards and behaviorist models of teacher evaluation and supervision. Teachers' efforts to rethink instruction in ways consistent with advances in cognitive science have been trumped by high-stakes accountability systems rooted in norm-reference tests. Teachers encountering an incoherent policy environment are apt to retreat to the quiet of their classrooms, rather than invest effort with their colleagues to reconsider practice and learn together.

Prospects for teacher communities to grow at the bottom of the system in schools and departments, and therefore our predictions for the future of teaching, depend upon changes at multiple levels of the system and upon their convergence in the work lives of teachers. Policy and leadership for teacher learning community builds around the core of teaching and learning and focuses on the quality of teachers' professional relationships. It excavates cultural deterrents to change and plants opportunities for teacher learning community and leadership. It countermands policies that conflict with goals of teacher learning and community (Darling-Hammond and McLaughlin 1999). The alignment of teaching and learning standards between systems, publics, and teacher communities is the challenge for the future of school-teaching.

Authorizing Professional Communities as Policy Systems

Fundamental to building strong learning communities in American high schools is locating within them collective authority and responsibility for decisions about how to conduct their work with students and colleagues. Currently, high schools and their subject departments exercise control over conditions of teaching that profoundly affect both students' and teachers' learning opportunities. They vary in how actively and collectively they do so and in how much guidance and support they take from the policy system and from professional associations. But despite the fact that professional communities are the ultimate makers of educational policy for their students, and mediators of the broader policy environment, they generally are neither granted authority nor held accountable for their decisions.[19]

Establishing a legitimate educational policy domain for high school subject departments and schools would engender teachers' mutual engagement and joint enterprise around instruction. These conditions are essential to the discourse and inquiry that sustain learning in a professional community. Moreover, formalizing teacher responsibility for core education might mitigate against the kinds of department policies that establish unequal student opportunities and achievements, since faculty decisions and rationale would be subject to public and peer scrutiny.

Consequential decisions that high school departments currently make informally suggest key elements of a policy domain for professional communities. They center on teaching practice—decisions about the connections within the classroom triangle of content-students-teacher—and around teacher learning opportunities and careers.

High school departments determine what courses are offered to which students. Underlying this important set of decisions are policy choices about how to organize a subject's curriculum—how to treat subtopics such as algebra and geometry in mathematics courses, whether and how to track courses, and what decision rules are used to assign students to courses. Such choices are only loosely constrained by district or state standards and policies, yet they effectively determine the educational opportunity structure for their students.

Moreover, high school communities set policy on how teachers are assigned to particular courses and students, further shaping students' learning opportunities. Such policy and assignment decisions are generally made by default of seniority or by department chair fiat, and they often work to exacerbate inequalities in student learning opportunities and outcomes. But they can be made in ways that promote equity when teachers take collective responsibility for all students' learning. Again, authorizing high school communities to make teacher assignment policy and decisions collectively is likely to engender shared responsibility and to reveal issues of equity that are otherwise hidden or ignored.

Teacher career policy is another promising decision domain around which to build high school learning community. If high schools were charged with developing policy and practice to support teacher learning in the course of day-to-day work, then considerations that are commonplace in teacher learning communities would come into focus. For example, it would be important to consider how novice teachers might learn with more experienced colleagues or how rotating courses might enhance professional growth. Teacher assignment policies might be seen in a new light when both teachers' and students' learning opportunities are taken into consideration. Responsibility to develop teaching policy and supports could be another way for high schools and departments to begin the work of learning in a professional community.

Little in the current zeitgeist of American public education promotes teachers' sense of agency or collective responsibility. The policy system casts high school teachers as implementers of higher-level standards and as accountable for student performance on norm-referenced tests that they had no say in designing or selecting. Thus, ironically, while high schools and their individual departments control fundamentally important educational decisions, teachers in them often feel powerless, and key decisions about teaching practice and careers are made without engaging the values and intelligence of professional communities.

Building teacher learning communities on a large scale across U.S. high schools will take more than exemplars, cultural drift toward principles compatible with innovative professional communities, and policy coherence at the top of the system. It will entail aligning professional authority with the reality of teacher communities' control over the work of high school teaching.

❦❦❦

The character and quality of teaching found in any high school classroom on any day signals much more than the attributes, energy, and expertise of an individual teacher. The work of high school teaching takes shape in professional communities— through norms for teaching, curriculum structures and assignment policies, collegial supports, and leadership messages about good professional practice. This observation pushes thinking about relations between policy resources and individual actions in new directions. Educators and researchers advance promising proposals for reform that move away from models, programs, or top-down solutions to center on increased support for teachers' learning and adaptation. We extend these propositions to locate the medium and foundation for that learning in teachers' professional communities.

Integrating Theory and Methods in Research on Teachers' Work

High school teachers' work is embedded in myriad school, community, and professional contexts. Our Center's research sought to understand how teachers make sense of the diverse and changing contexts of their work and how those contexts matter for teaching practice and careers. In order to capture diverse and embedded contexts of teaching, we designed a research program that departs in many ways from conventional educational research practice. Here we explain the theoretical and methodological choices that underlie this book's findings and comment on ways that our decisions break rules of social science tradition. We offer design criteria that meet research goals of both understanding teachers' lived realities and informing education policy.

MULTIPLE LENSES ON EMBEDDED
TEACHING CONTEXTS

Sociological research on schoolteaching typically focuses on a particular teaching context through a particular theoretical lens. For example, studies using an institutional theory, or cultural, perspective document ways in which social class cultures find their way into classrooms and schools (Anyon 1980; Metz 1990a) or investigate how subject cultures frame teaching practice

(Grossman and Stodolsky 1995). Studies using organization systems theory estimate effects of private school status and school organization on students' test performance (Coleman and Hoffer 1987; Lee and Bryk 1989) or examine how school organization and redesign affect teachers' work (see Smylie 1994 for a review). Studies using social systems theory consider the ways in which professional norms and communities of practice shape teachers' work lives (Little 1982, 1990; Cochran-Smith and Lytle 1999; Stein, Silver, and Smith 1998). Our research seeks dialogue among these perspectives and the kinds of contexts they highlight so that we can see teaching more completely.

Institutional Environments

Teaching contexts outside of school systems, such as subject cultures and higher education, comprise the broad and diverse institutional environments of K–12 schooling.[1] We find that such contexts are among the most important in high school teaching, where the work of teachers generally is specialized by subject. Subject disciplines not only carry different beliefs about learning and teaching (chapter 3), but their effective institutional and policy contexts differ. For example, academic and nonacademic classes within the same school have different institutional environments. Academic subjects and classes are affected by institutions such as college entrance requirements and SAT and AP exams, while local labor markets and economic conditions can be a powerful frame for teaching in nonacademic classes.[2]

Students' family and community cultures also constitute primary institutional contexts of teaching. These contexts differ across schools and also within schools that track students from diverse cultural backgrounds. We selected a school sample for our study that includes private and suburban schools serving students from middle-class, well-educated families; inner-city schools serving a majority of poor students of color; and urban schools serving students from widely diverse social class, race/ethnic, and language cultural contexts (see appendix B). Growing economic inequality in American society exacerbates contrasts in the socioeconomic contexts of teachers' work within and between schools. These elements of the institutional environment are highly salient to teachers and constitute key parameters of their work.

Administrative Contexts

The organizational system, or administrative, contexts of schooling are what researchers generally consider as setting the conditions of teachers' work. Researchers tend to focus on one or another level of the administrative system of K–12 schools to analyze educational policies, programs, and resources for teaching. Our schema distinguishes state and district policy contexts from the proximate school and classroom settings of teachers' work. Within most high schools, the subject department is another key formal unit of school organization (Siskin 1994), though the current restructuring movement promotes new kinds of organizational units such as houses" and "cottages" and "small learning communities" to create a smaller scale and more continuity for student-adult relations. Our study analyzes teachers' work within fairly typical school organization structures and considers ways in which conditions in multiple administrative levels shape teachers' daily work and careers (chapter 5).

Social Systems Contexts

A third theoretical lens views teachers' work in its social systems contexts, examining collegial relations and social norms in teachers' daily work lives. In our research, we came to understand teacher communities—networks of teachers in subject departments or schools—as the primary contexts of teaching. As social systems, they construct and maintain cultures that frame professional practice and interpret particular institutional and administrative conditions of teaching (chapters 2–3). These proximate social systems of schooling—differing in strength and culture—mediate the effects of broader educational contexts on teachers' work (chapter 5).

Figure A.1 illustrates the kinds of contexts we have outlined in this study. The proximate contexts of teachers' work lives in school settings of classes, professional community, and school are embedded within the broader organization system and institutional contexts. A single theoretical framework and more limited analytic model would miss the embedded character of these high school teaching contexts.

Our conception of the teaching environment as embedded contexts departs from a more common view that school contexts are nested—that is, hierarchical in structure and additive in their

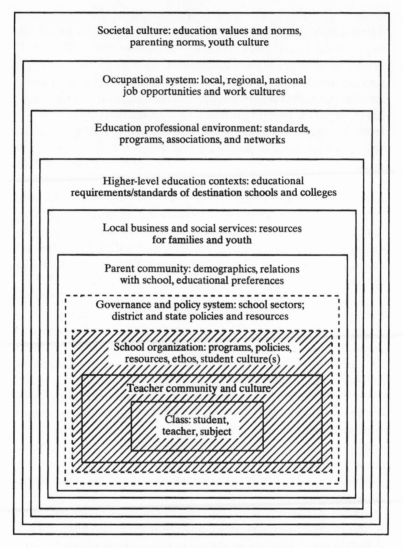

Societal culture: education values and norms,
parenting norms, youth culture

Occupational system: local, regional, national
job opportunities and work cultures

Education professional environment: standards,
programs, associations, and networks

Higher-level education contexts: educational
requirements/standards of destination schools and colleges

Local business and social services: resources
for families and youth

Parent community: demographics, relations
with school, educational preferences

Governance and policy system: school sectors;
district and state policies and resources

School organization: programs, policies,
resources, ethos, student culture(s)

Teacher community and culture

Class: student,
teacher, subject

KEY:

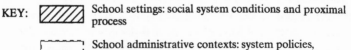

School settings: social system conditions and proximal
process

School administrative contexts: system policies,
resources, structures

Institutional contexts: local community and broader
educational environment

Figure A.1   Multiple and Embedded Settings and Contexts of Schooling

effects on educational processes. We assume interactive and transactive relationships among school settings and contexts in their effects on teachers' work.

The notion that "micro" settings of daily school life are embedded in "macro" contexts of schooling at a higher analytic level suggests that macro conditions, such as institutional norms and cultures, are experienced directly in school settings. In this view, the proximal education settings of classes, teacher communities, and schools are permeated by the contexts in which they are embedded. Elements of educational culture from multiple school contexts are incorporated, or enacted, by individuals in school settings. This phenomenon accounts for commonalities observed across school settings, such as administrative structures (Meyer and Rowan 1977), ways of organizing instruction into age groups and grade levels, and modes of teaching. It also accounts for differences across schools that derive from differences in their social class or ethnic cultures or district administrative cultures, for example. In this sense of embeddedness, cultural contexts of schooling are embedded in teachers' work.

Second, the notion of embedded contexts accommodates our research finding that teacher communities located in the same objective student population, school organization, district administration, and state policy system can forge substantively different professional cultures. Effects of the broader contexts and conditions of schooling are socially mediated within proximal school settings; they are not transmitted directly and evenly by higher-level organization units to lower-level units, as a nested model assumes. An embedded-context framework assumes that multiple context conditions are interpreted and acted upon by social groups in subject departments and other school settings. In this meaning, teachers' work is embedded in multiple contexts, the salience and significance of which are socially defined.

Finally, our view of the school environment highlights the possibility that different combinations of context conditions have qualitatively different impacts on teachers' work. The notion of embedded contexts invites analyses of the interactive effects of multiple school conditions. How do various context conditions combine to affect teaching practices? The notion of embedded contexts cautions against assumptions of additivity implicit in much of the school-effects research. Attention to context means more than measuring conditions and assessing their average effects on teaching and learning; it means looking at effects of coincident conditions. In this sense, the significance of a particular condition, or a context effect on teachers' work, is embedded in other context conditions.

INTEGRATING RESEARCH METHODS

A multilens conceptual approach to research on teaching calls for an integration of methodological traditions. In specialized research traditions, methods align with focus. Research on institutional patterns or "constancies" of teachers' work tends to use ethnographic methods and case studies, while research on organizational effects generally uses survey research methods. Such traditions describe the coincident realities of teachers' work lives, but they fail to capture their interdependencies.

A research design to assess multiple, embedded environments of teaching and learning departs in some important respects from conventions of behavioral science research. Not only does it go beyond typical analytic boundaries and theoretical traditions of educational research, but it breaks norms for social science research methods in both quantitative and qualitative traditions. For example, instead of sampling on one unit of analysis to ensure breadth and case independence or focusing intensively on a particular case, an embedded context model calls for substantial numbers of interdependent cases. In order to ensure that their dialogue will reveal both broad patterns and insights into critical cases, neither the quantitative nor the qualitative research tradition is placed in a subservient position.

General Research Strategies

Fundamental to embedded-context research are questions of which levels and how those different levels or units of analysis are relevant to particular substantive and theoretical issues regarding teachers' work. For example, how is teachers' commitment to the profession shaped by district contracts and culture, or by school conditions, or by teachers' professional community? We treat the unit-of-analysis problem as an important empirical question in any line of inquiry. The capacity to detect which contexts and conditions matter for a criterion of interest depends upon strategic choices in sampling and what we refer to as a "bottom-up" approach to measurement and analysis. As a line of analysis on teaching progresses, particular levels and cases within them become important.

The notion of integrated research methods typically connotes the use of both quantitative and qualitative measurement techniques, such as surveys and interviews, quantitative scales and qualitative codes, standardized and unstandardized data collection. Combining quantitative and qualitative measures of teachers' work is certainly included in our meaning of integrative methods. However, our notion of methodological integration refers especially to combining, simultaneously and iteratively, what Charles Ragin (1987) referred to as "variable-oriented" and "case-oriented" research. This distinction crosscuts quantitative and qualitative measurement techniques; indeed, we recommend using qualitative and quantitative measures in both kinds of analysis.

A serious treatment of the distinction between variable-oriented and case-oriented research is beyond the scope of this appendix. It juxtaposes broad methodological traditions of sociological research, each with its own family of problems and means of addressing them (for extensive discussion, see Ragin 1987; Ragin and Becker 1992). Their distinctive purposes and strategies are summarized in table A.1.

Most simply, variable-oriented research analyzes the covariance of particular phenomena across large numbers of cases, while case-oriented research analyzes the coincidence of phenomena within a particular site or a selected set of sites. Of course, the cases for either kind of research on teaching could be individual teachers, classes, departments, schools, states, nations, and so on. The variable-oriented approach is valuable in isolating school organizational and social system variables that underlie differences in the character and quality of teachers' professional lives and practices; its primary weakness is in the decontextualized generalizations it yields. The case-oriented approach illuminates constancies in teaching, meanings of embedded context conditions, and processes by which contexts affect teachers' work; a weakness is the particularized generalizations it yields and the unknown relation of case(s) to their popula-

Table A.1 Methods of Social Science Research: Variable-Oriented vs. Case-Oriented Approaches

	Variable-Oriented Methods	Case-Oriented Methods
Analytic focus	Covariation of conditions across many cases; probabalistic relations	Syndrome of conditions within cases(s); patterns common to cases
Substantive interest	Factors that influence variation in phenomena of interest	Constancies and case contrasts in phenomena of interest
Research strategy	Sample surveys and multivariate analyses	Intensive field research
Standards for research		
Samples	Random samples, independent cases	Purposive sample; embedded settings
Measures	Predetermined unit(s) and variables for analysis; standard quantitative measures	Case-based measures and meanings of phenomena
Analyses	Focus on relationships between variables across cases; statistical controls for "confounding" variables	Focus on coincidence of conditions, patterns within cases

tions. Our embedded-context research design allows for strategic integration of the two approaches to achieve a contextually rich understanding of teachers' work.

Sampling Strategies

Quantitative research standards call for sampling designs to ensure independent cases for analysis. The nationally representative samples of students and schools established for national education longitudinal studies maximize dispersion of school environments and are considered by many to be ideal for estimating context effects on educational outcomes, if not for providing rich measures of context conditions. These samples provide good estimates of population parameters for U.S. schools on survey variables. However, they provide limited opportunity to study how environments of schooling affect teaching and learning. This is because context variables under analysis have been extracted from their own contexts. Indeed, analyses in the school-effects tradition statistically control for confounded context variables and rarely look for interaction effects. Our conceptual model of the school environment challenges this standard and calls for samples of embedded contexts.

An embedded-context sample design aims to capture important local contrasts within the context of important higher-level contrasts. Ideally, researchers would study large samples of teachers within a large number of contrasting school settings and contrasting policy contexts. Given limited resources, however, researchers face important tradeoffs between sample size and capacity to measure and analyze conditions of the multiple, embedded contexts represented in the sample. What kind of manageable sample provides the best opportunity to understand context effects on teaching? How many and what kinds of cases are needed in particular school settings and contexts?

At the proximate levels of the school environment, large numbers of teachers at grade levels, curricular tracks, departments, and school settings are essential to ensure that common and different conditions of teachers' work are captured in interviews and surveys. It is this daily variation in teachers' practice and experience of context that research on teachers' work seeks to explain. Dense samples within settings are essential for the kinds of analyses we propose.

Selecting higher-level cases is purposive and aims to represent contrasts on context variables of particular theoretical and practical importance. The question of numbers of higher-level cases therefore depends upon contrasts that are important for lines of inquiry, as well as upon research resources. Given limited degrees of freedom for higher-level context sampling, the selection of contrasts to represent in an embedded-context study is a core issue for theory and design. A particular sampling frame sets constraints and capacities for the kinds of analyses and insights possible in a study of teachers' work.

Our longitudinal study included all teachers in sixteen school sites, located in seven different districts, in four metropolitan areas, in two states (see appendix B). We chose "locations" to establish contrasts on potentially important dimensions of teachers' embedded contexts. This sample enabled us to observe differences in teachers' work experiences between state and district school systems, while looking at comparable school settings; and, conversely, we could analyze differences between subject department settings within a particular district and state school system. We were thus able to tease out ways in which the state policy environments mattered for teachers' daily work, for example. We observed that the California mathematics framework enabled high school math teachers to consider ways of adapting instructional practices to meet their students' needs. Michigan teachers, on the other hand, were not pushed to examine practice and lacked the opportunities for learning new content and pedagogy that had been generated by the California reform framework. Multiple sites within a district afforded a similar window on the effects of a local system across diverse teaching settings. For example, we saw that teachers in very different schools and departments shared views on their district's professionalism, or how well the district was supporting teacher learning and commitment (chapter 5).

An embedded-sampling design is never able to capture all important context variables or their combinations. However, it offers perspective on the embeddedness of teachers' work in multiple settings and contexts—a perspective that is lost in both large random samples of schools and in-depth case studies.

Measurement Strategies

Our approach to measuring teachers' work contexts combines sustained and iterative quantitative and qualitative research in a large field sample of schools, with "bridging" analyses to survey data for large representative teacher samples.[3] Figure A.2 summarizes these general research strategies.

The first strategy is important for assessing the relevance and substantive significance of particular contexts for teachers' work and for directing case studies concerned with particular teaching conditions. The second strategy—of bridging samples and data from the embedded-context study with national survey samples and data—provides a way to evaluate sampling and effect-estimate biases and, so, to overcome weaknesses and limitations of a purposive field sample.

A longitudinal, iterative approach to developing survey and interview data for a large field sample aims to achieve the depth of understanding of particular school sites that ethnographic methods afford for small numbers of sites and the breadth of

LONGITUDINAL FIELD
RESEARCH

NATIONAL SURVEY
SAMPLES AND DATA

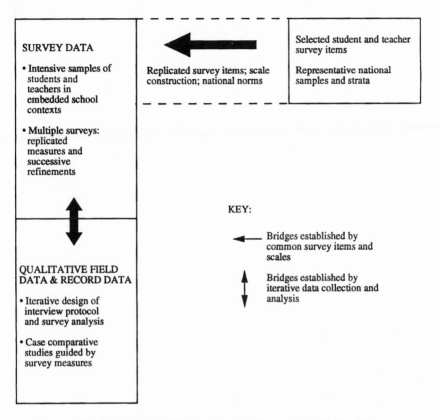

SURVEY DATA

• Intensive samples of
students and
teachers in
embedded school
contexts

• Multiple surveys:
replicated
measures and
successive
refinements

Replicated survey items; scale
construction; national norms

Selected student and teacher
survey items

Representative national
samples and strata

**QUALITATIVE FIELD
DATA & RECORD DATA**

• Iterative design of
interview protocol
and survey analysis

• Case comparative
studies guided by
survey measures

KEY:

Bridges established by
common survey items and
scales

Bridges established by
iterative data collection and
analysis

Figure A.2 Strategies for Bridging Quantitative and Qualitative Measures
of School Context

understanding that survey methods afford. Successive rounds of
interviews in each site turn up common and unique themes
across sites and identify conditions that distinguish each site. For
instance, we learned in the first year of our sixteen-school study
that the principals whom teachers rated as strong leaders, according to survey scores, played very different roles in teachers'
work lives across school sites; principal leadership had substantively different meanings in schools with comparably high scores
on the survey scale. Iterative development of survey instruments

refined measures of teachers' work and quantitative portraits of school and department cases and also served to focus interviews and qualitative data analysis.

Our strategy of bridging field and large-scale survey data addresses endemic problems of field-based research, especially the issue of how well a particular field sample captures tendencies and variability in a population. By replicating selected items from national teacher surveys in our field surveys, we have been able to measure teaching conditions in our field sample against national norms. We see, for example, how differences in teacher collegiality that we found between subject departments in a high school compare to national norms for the respective subjects (see chapter 3). We also plot principal leadership ratings in our sample against national norms both to judge the significance of differences in means across our cases and to evaluate the range of context that we captured in our field sample (chapter 5). This measurement strategy overcomes some of the limitations of purposive sampling in field research and considerably extends the analytic capacity of field research in embedded teaching contexts.

Analysis Strategies: Moving between Variables and Cases
We use a "bottom-up strategy" to describe context effects on teachers' work. This term has two meanings: as perspective on context and as analytic approach to assessing context effects. In the first meaning, we highlight the role of teachers' subjective perceptions of school context conditions. While we recommend that researchers also obtain measures of context from record data and administrators, where reliable, we emphasize the key role of perceptions in framing individuals' actions. Especially in loosely coupled settings like schools (Bidwell 1965; Weick 1976; Meyer and Rowan 1977), individuals and groups construct salient realities to a significant degree. We found, for example, that teachers in urban school settings varied substantially in their perceptions of the academic potential of the same students; in some schools, we observed large differences between subject departments on such measures (chapter 3).

The notion of bottom-up inquiry also refers to strategies for determining unit(s) for analysis in ongoing research. Rather than deciding a priori which level of analysis to adopt for a given study, the researcher treats this as an empirical question by using multiple levels of aggregation for individual data on criteria measures. Internal variability at any level of analysis is treated as a problem of identifying new units for analysis, rather than as a problem of reliability. The empirical issue is this: Across what level/units of analysis, or kind of schooling context, do we observe systematic variation in particular facets of teachers' work?

With field samples of the sort described here, we then look to the data to detect which cases account for a pattern. Are there distinct subsamples of cases that show a kind of context effect? For example, we observed that most of the between-school variance in our sixteen-school sample on measures of collegiality was produced by high values for the independent and public mission high schools in our study. For comprehensive public schools, as it turned out, variance in collegiality was mainly between departments. This bottom-up strategy identifies which kind or level of context matters for a particular variable, using subjective survey data and objective boundaries of school settings and contexts. Analyses of variance on survey measures also identify cases within those contexts that deviate from the general patterns. The cases that we highlight in this book emerged through such analyses to be strategic sites for understanding proximate settings of teaching within comparable organization and institutional contexts of teaching.

The Research Sample

The multiple kinds and levels of high school teaching contexts jointly shape both the classroom core and the resources of teachers' work. For example, education policy frameworks influence curricula and accountability; communities bring particular expectations for student learning and performance; schools lend physical, social, and material definition to teaching; students bring their knowledge, interests, and needs into the classroom. The states, districts, and schools selected for this study were chosen to provide contrasts on those dimensions of teachers' multiple workplace contexts that research or policy highlight as significant influences on schoolteaching.

STATE AND LOCAL POLICY CONTEXTS

Does the education policy context matter to schoolteachers, or are teachers, insulated inside their classrooms, largely indifferent to the policies swirling outside, as generations of research on education change and policy implementation suggest? Systemic reformers who advocate national, state, and local standards and frameworks for instruction and assessment assume the former. However, some researchers point to the historically weak link between policy and practice as reasons to expect that even coherent, well-articulated policies at state or district levels will not penetrate classrooms to affect practice in a consistent, meaningful way (see Cohen and Spillane 1993).

State Policy Contexts

State policy systems provide a broad canvas for public education, and they have changed dramatically in the last quarter century. The states' role in public education was at best that of bit actor prior to the 1965 passage of the Elementary and Secondary Education Act when federal policies enlisted states as junior partners in the task of improving public education through categorical education initiatives (Murphy 1974; McDonnell and McLaughlin 1982). In the next two decades, the simultaneous forces of federal policy decentralization through President Ronald Reagan's New Federalism, and the state centralization of local finance through school finance reform and taxpayer revolts (such as that begun in 1978 by California's Proposition 13) boosted states' substantive and fiscal authority. For all of these reasons, state Departments of Education function today both as a source and a conduit of reform as state initiatives in such key areas as curriculum, teacher credentials, and assessment have gathered momentum and federally sponsored reforms have assigned responsibility for definition and oversight to the states.[1]

The state policy contexts for this study—California and Michigan—differed in many important ways during the period of our research. In the late 1980s, Michigan still had a highly decentralized education system. In contrast, California had a history of reform and state-level authority in education. California's centralized educational finance provided roughly 60 percent of local education funds. The state was a leader in implementing standards-based reforms and curricula frameworks. For example, its 1985 mathematics framework was precursor for the National Council of Teachers of Mathematics' standards document. Teachers in Michigan's decentralized education system experienced little state role in education during the late 1980s.

District Policy Contexts

Although the district was once the dominant context of local education, joint forces of expanded state control of local finances in some states, like California, and increased federal and state emphasis on policies that bypass the district to target the school (categorical programs, charter schools, site-based management initiatives, public or private choice plans, for example) have moved the district to the background as a policy actor.[2] Perhaps this low visibility explains why the district has received relatively little attention from researchers (Crowson 1990; Lusi 1997). Researchers who have examined the district role, however, reach mixed conclusions about its consequence for classrooms. Richard Elmore (1993), for example, finds little evidence that districts have ever played a significant role in educational improvement (see also Hill and Bonan 1991). Robert Floden and his colleagues (1988) characterize the district's role in teaching and instruction as largely equivocal; it has neither supported teachers' autonomy to make decisions about instruction nor provided clear guidance about classroom practices.

Other accounts, however, suggest that districts can and do matter for schoolteaching. Susan Rosenholtz (1989) distinguishes between "stuck" and "moving" school districts. The former are relatively fragmented in their goals for schools, instructional policies, and priorities for practice. Moving districts, in contrast, provide clear focus for administrators and teachers, bring coherence to instruction, and keep up to date with current thinking about best practice. Moving districts generally have more resources than stuck districts. Moreover, these district differences, according to Rosenholtz, are reflected at the school and teacher levels; stuck districts have disproportionately more stuck schools while moving districts have more schools with high levels of innovation and reform activity and more teachers with high levels of commitment.

Consistent with these data, other researchers find that districts do affect instructional practices when administrators establish clear priorities for teaching and learning and then align elements of the instructional system to support those goals— particularly in the area of teachers' professional development (Murphy and Hallinger 1988; Spillane 1996; see also Fullan 1993). Research also shows that district leadership can make a difference in the way state and national reform efforts are interpreted locally. For example, researchers from the Consortium for Policy Research in Education (CPRE) find that districts already committed to the goals articulated in their state's reform agenda consistently meet or exceed state requirements in areas of restructuring and standards-based reform (Firestone, Fuhrman, and Kirst 1989).

Our sample of seven school districts provides opportunity to pursue questions about district significance for teaching. It represents contrasts along many of the key dimensions thought to distinguish districts as a professional workplace—size, community setting, degree of involvement in curricular policies, support for teachers' professional development, and superintendents' commitment to reform. Our sample ranges from a very small suburban district to sprawling urban systems, from relatively homogeneous middle-class communities to districts that embrace a broad ethnic and social class diversity (see table B.1).

The districts in our sample comprise two distinct professional contexts. Three of our districts—Adobe and Oak Valley in California and Dover in Michigan—are "moving" in terms of their clear objectives for education, reform and priorities for teachers' professionalism. The remaining four were "stuck," and paid little attention to innovation and reform.

Table B.1 School Sample Characteristics

	Region	Sector/District	Size[a]
California Schools[b]			
Scholastic (01)	Mostaza	Mostaza	S
Esperanza (02)	Mostaza	Mostaza	L
Rancho (03)	Mostaza	Mostaza	L
Greenfield (04)	Mostaza	Independent	S
Paloma (05)	Mostaza	Independent	S
Valley (06)	Adobe Viejo	Adobe Viejo	M
Onyx Ridge (07)	Adobe Viejo	Adobe Viejo	M
Ibsen (08)	Adboe Viejo	Adobe Viejo	M
Oak Valley (10)	Adobe Viejo	Oak Valley	XL
Juliet Wright (09)	Adobe Viejo	Independent	S
Michigan Schools			
Highlander (12)	Burton	Burton	XL
Washington Academy (13)	Burton	Burton	L
Dover (11)	Burton	Dover	L
LaSalle (15)	Falls Park	Falls Park	M
Monroe (16)	Falls Park	Falls Park	S
Prospect (14)	Falls Park	Oneida	S

[a] Sizes are reported in ranges based on the school's student enrollment in 1988–89: S = <885; M = 885–1500; L = 1,501–2,075; XL = >2,075.
[b] Schools are listed by their pseudonym and code number.

School Sector

Research and conventional wisdom have attributed different teaching and learning outcomes to differences in the organizational environments of public and private schools (see, for example, Scott and Meyer 1994). James Coleman and Thomas Hoffer (1987), for example, argued that the strong school communities of private schools promote student achievement. Anthony Bryk, Valerie Lee, and Peter Holland (1993) estimated that the personalized school environments of Catholic schools were a significant factor explaining why children attending parochial schools outperform similar students attending public schools. Arthur Powell (1990, 1996) compared the workplace conditions of teachers in independent schools with those of their public school colleagues and found that teachers' experience of effectiveness was associated with their autonomy and responsibility, conditions more prevalent in the private sector. Theodore Sizer described the debilitating effects of public school bureaucracy on high school teachers, such as Horace, the beleaguered teacher portrayed in *Horace's Compromise* (1984).

Less clear in these and other reports, however, is the extent to which these differences in organizational arrangements are explained by fundamental conditions that distinguish private and public schools. John Chubb and Terry Moe (1990) argued that market forces and the absence of a public bureaucracy make private schools more responsive to parent wishes and easier to operate. However, other accounts focus on internal features of private schools that at least theoretically could be replicated in the public sector. For example, average differences in personalization between sectors could be equalized by public school policies that reduce class size and leadership to promote student-centered teaching and learning.

We included three very different private schools in our sample in order to explore such questions about the significance of sector for teachers' work—Paloma, Juliet Wright, and Greenfield, all located in California. Paloma, an elite college preparatory school, educates young women headed for prestigious colleges and universities, notable careers, and lives of leadership and social responsibility. Juliet Wright, a college preparatory school turned down a notch from Paloma's academic intensity, enrolls an "intellectually heterogeneous" student population and prides itself on providing a "personalized" alternative to the public schools. Greenfield frames its mission in sharply contrasting terms. Established for youth who, in the words of the head, "say school sucks," Greenfield aims to connect students to school and productive futures. Each of these private schools finds a rough counterpart in our sample of public schools and allows us to explore the role of sector in high school teaching.

School Organization and Community Context

Researchers, policy makers, parents, and students point to school conditions they believe matter for teaching and learning. School size tops many parent and student lists of conditions that affect what goes on in school and how students feel about their experience there. In terms of sheer physical size, the schools in our sample range from the very large (Oak Valley and its more than 3,000 students) to the very small (Greenfield and Prospect, both of which enroll around 120 students). While many parents, teachers, and students say that size alone makes a difference to the feel and function of a school, researchers point to other aspects of a school that may be, but are not necessarily, size related. Among them are the fit between teachers' goals and the goals of the school, a sense of clear school charter or mission, organizational complexity related to instructional tracks and specialization, and the extent to which a school environment is a personal one.[3]

The three independent schools in our sample, Paloma, Juliet Wright, and Greenfield, as well as the special-mission public schools, Ibsen and Prospect, provide opportunity to explore the significance of clear school mission and teachers' identification with school goals. Each of these schools signals strong school identity and purpose. The large comprehensive high schools in our sample—Esperanza, Rancho, Valley, Oak Valley, Onyx Ridge, Highlander, Monroe, and LaSalle—provide instances of complex school organizations that differ in such respects as personalized environment, professional satisfaction, and teachers' commitment to students.

Other school contexts that researchers and policy makers hold important to teaching center on students and their families. For example, the relationship between student achievement and parental social class and education has been a consis-

Table B.2 Academic Achievement, Socioeconomic Status, and Ethnic Composition of California Public High School Sample, 1991–92 School Year

District/School[a]	Academically Advanced Students[b]	Poor Students[c] (%)	Minority Students[d] (%)
Mostaza District		20–29	60–69
Scholastic	10–19	40–49	60–69
Esperanza	20–29	20–29	50–59
Rancho	20–29	20–29	50–59
Adobe Viejo District		30–39	60–69
Valley	20–29	30–39	50–59
Onyx Ridge	60–69	10–19	40–49
Ibsen	40–49	20–29	40–49
Oak Valley District		0–9	20–29
Oak Valley	40–49	0–9	10–19

[a] School data are reported as ranges to ensure school anonymity.
[b] Percentage of graduating seniors meeting University of California A–F entrance requirements and thus eligible for admission to top-tier state universities.
[c] Percentage of students eligible for the free or reduced-price lunch program.
[d] Percentage of students who are nonwhite or Hispanic.

Table B.3 Academic Achievement, Socioeconomic Status, and Ethnic Composition of Michigan Public High School Sample, 1991–92 School Year

District/School[a]	Academically Satisfactory Students[b]			Poor Students[c] (%)	Minority Students[d] (%)
	Math	Reading	Science		
Burton District				40–49	60–69
Highlander	0–9	10–19	10–19	30–39	80–89
Washington Academy	10–19	30–39	20–29	10–19	60–69
Dover District				0–10	0–10
Dover High School	20–29	40–49	40–49	0–10	0–10
Falls Park District				50–59	50–59
LaSalle	10–19	30–39	30–39	20–29	40–49
Monroe	0–10	20–29	10–19	40–49	50–59
Oneida District				20–29	0–10
Prospect	n.a.	10–19	30–39	n.a.	n.a.

[a] School data are reported as ranges to ensure school anonymity.
[b] Percentage of tenth-grade students testing "satisfactory" on the Michigan Educational Assessment Program (MEAP).
[c] Percentage of students eligible for the free or reduced-price lunch program.
[d] Percentage of students who are nonwhite or Hispanic.

tent theme in research aimed at explaining differential levels of student achievement.[4] The communities served by our sample schools range from generally well-educated and middle-class families (Onyx Ridge, Oak Valley, Dover, Paloma, Juliet Wright, and Greenfield) to those with both middle-class and poor families (Esperanza, Rancho, Scholastic, Ibsen, Valley, Washington Academy, and LaSalle) to those with generally poor families (Monroe, Prospect, and Highlander). Student economic and cultural characteristics also have been found to affect teachers' attitudes and practices. For example, one line of research finds that the culture and diversity of a school's student body often plays a role in defining teachers' satisfaction and sense of professional effectiveness.[5] Our school sample provides a rich opportunity to explore the significance of student diversity for teachers' work (see tables B.2 and B.3).

❦❦❦

The private and public schools we studied each had a distinctive professional culture and organizational character. Here we provide a brief description of each of the schools and districts in our sample. All of these cases are included in comparative, cross-case analyses of teacher survey and interview data; however, some become the focus of school or department cases studies because they stand out in the comparative analysis as representing particular conditions or contrasts within a common system context. For example, math departments in Rancho and Esperanza are featured because their professional communities contrast significantly, yet they share a district and state policy context. Greenfield and Prospect are interesting cases for comparison, since they have developed very similar schoolwide professional communities to meet the needs of their similar student clientele, yet they differ in all other respects—sector, social class of clientele, state and local policy context. The reader will thus come to know some of these schools more than others.

THE INDEPENDENT SCHOOLS

The three independent schools in our sample, introduced above, are Paloma, Juliet Wright, and Greenfield.

Paloma. Paloma is an archetypal college preparatory school. This all-girls, nonsectarian, 7–12 school has evolved from a finishing school for debutantes to an elite academic institution. Small school and class size allow a high degree of personalization and individual attention. Parents are involved and supportive, although faculty members feel that too many parents see Paloma only as a ticket to a select university. The girls are heavily scheduled with academic, extracurricular, and volunteer activities; academics are seen in high-stakes terms by both students and their affluent parents. All of Paloma's students are college bound, and a high percentage of them go on to prestigious colleges and universities.

Juliet Wright. Although Juliet Wright also is college preparatory, it is not as demanding academically as Paloma. The pre-K through 12 school is divided into lower, middle, and upper schools. In administrator's terms, students' abilities in the upper school range from "average on up." Juliet Wright distinguishes itself as a "family" school and emphasizes total family involvement, individually tailored college counseling and a personalized, supportive educational environment. Juliet Wright students are predominately European American and from affluent families. All seniors are accepted into a college and most go directly on to college.

Greenfield. Greenfield, the third independent school in our sample, frames its mission in very different terms than do Paloma and Juliet Wright. Greenfield was established for youth who have failed in other settings. Greenfield aims to enable its students to take responsibility for their lives and learning and move to a positive future. Many of the school's predominately European-American students have been in and out of various institutions—juvenile justice or mental health—and a significant number struggle with substance abuse or unstable family circumstances. Faculty members characterize their students as emotionally fragile, turned off, and tuned out and work together as a tight community to construct an educational environment that fosters their engagement and success.

All three independent schools are in California; Paloma and Greenfield are in the Mostaza metropolitan area; Juliet Wright is in Adobe Viejo. They differ in their educational missions, clientele, and expectations for faculty and students. Since our sample includes public schools with comparable missions and clientele, we are able to assess the role of sector in shaping the high schools' organizational ethos and conditions of teachers' work.

CALIFORNIA DISTRICTS AND SCHOOLS

We studied schools in three California districts with differing community contexts and character: Mostaza, Adobe Viejo, and Oak Valley.

Mostaza Unified School District

Mostaza, located in one of California's counties most affected by immigration, was "typical" of many California districts in the diversity of its students' language, culture, and family circumstances. It ranks among the top quarter of California districts in terms of enrollment of "limited English proficient" students. The district spans more than twenty miles, comprising an inner-city neighborhood of aging bungalows and inexpensive apartments as well as mid-city neighborhoods that have seen successive waves of working-class and professional families and newer, expensive areas primarily housing young Anglo families. Like many other California districts, Mostaza's student population had become "majority minority" by the early 1990s.

The Mostaza district had been locked in a long, difficult struggle to desegregate its schools. A desegregation settlement in the mid-1980s abruptly and drastically changed the ethnic, linguistic, and socioeconomic composition of Mostaza's classrooms almost overnight. Radical change in students' school assignments took place in the context of acrimonious labor relations. A bitter teachers' strike and charges of broken promises for salary increases led Mostaza teachers' to a "work to rule" posture just as the district was wrestling with the details of its complicated desegregation plan. Mostaza ceded autonomy on both fronts: declared bankruptcy brought the district under the surveillance of state auditors, and a federal court assumed direct control of district desegregation plans. Severe budgetary constraints exacerbated the district's poor relations with the teachers' union; the district was forced to turn contract disputes over to external arbiters.

Perhaps because of these pressures on district administrators and resources, Mostaza had not developed coherent policies about instruction or teachers' professional development. District reform efforts had been piecemeal, one area of instruction, and then another. They did not represent clearly articulated district priorities, either for Mostaza schools overall or for individual disciplines. Clearly, district energies had been focused elsewhere. The district desegregation struggles had a profound impact on each of the three schools we studied in Mostaza— Scholastic, Esperanza, and Rancho.

Scholastic. Scholastic, located in Mostaza's poorest area and in one of California's oldest public high school buildings, was transformed from an essentially all-minority school to a more racially balanced student body. Mostaza officials designated Scholastic as an academic magnet to attract European-American students across town. Prior to the district's court-ordered desegregation (1985), the student body was 95 percent minority and academic performance was poor. Overall test scores were among the lowest in the state. By the fall of 1989, approximately 50 percent of Scholastic functioned as an academic academy, while the rest of the school offered less ambitious fare. A pioneer spirit exists among teachers at Scholastic, especially among those working in the academic magnet courses.

Esperanza. Esperanza, a comprehensive high school serving grades 9–12, also was transformed by sudden shifts in student demographics resulting from the twin forces of court-ordered desegregation and immigration. Esperanza, a "premiere" Mostaza school in the 1960s, a decade later had lost many of its neighborhood students to Rancho (described below), built nearby in the mid-1970s. The most profound changes in Esperanza's student body, however, occurred in the 1980s in response to court-ordered desegregation. Between 1986 and 1988, the composition of the Esperanza student body changed from 92 percent local middle-class European-American youth, to 58 percent largely low-income ethnic minority students, with a third of the student population bused in from several miles away. Whereas only a handful of students were learning English as a second language in the mid-1980s, in 1990–91, almost one-third of the students in the school were classified as having limited or no proficiency in English. Transiency was a "horrendous" problem at Esperanza, according to teachers and administrators. Esperanza's experienced, predominately European-American faculty encountered a minority student population for the first time in their careers. Under the leadership of Esperanza's administrative team, this challenge was framed as an opportunity to rethink school policies and practices. This positive response to the school's changed student population earned the school a reputation as a "good place to work," and the faculty are praised for a "can do" spirit.

Rancho. Rancho, located a few miles down the road from Esperanza, also struggled to serve a newly diverse student body. Situated in a newer, upper-middle-class neighborhood, Rancho faculty saw its predominately white, middle-class student body change in 1986. A new student population, primarily Latino and Asian, came to Rancho from downtown Mostaza; between 1985 and 1990, minority student enrollment increased from 20 percent to 50 percent. Rancho's 1990–91 WASC report characterized the school as "in a transitory state." During the period of our study, Rancho had three different principals and a revolving cadre of assistant principals. This administrative instability, along with district turbulence, has eroded the structural features developed to further Rancho's founding mission. (Rancho opened in 1976 with an express student-centered mission and a house structure intended to promote personalization and a sense of learning community.) Nevertheless, Rancho has remained relatively popular within Mostaza as a place to work "because it's large, has lots of facilities for teachers, more chances to try something different or new, it's aesthetically pleasing." However, in contrast to Esperanza during the 1988–91 period, Rancho's school community has little cohesion, leadership, or warrant to rethink practices in the context of their changed student population.

Adobe Viejo School District

As in the Mostaza region, people who live in the sprawling Adobe Viejo metropolitan area represent a wide range of socio-economic levels and cultures. The hills and coastal neighborhoods of Adobe Viejo are home to extremely wealthy, predominately Anglo families; working class and transitional households live in the next ring of the city; the inner city houses most of area's ethnic minority population—Latinos and Southeast Asians predominate. An African-American community sits in one corner of the city. In the periphery, suburban communities such as Oak Valley grew by leaps and bounds during the 1970s and 1980s as middle-class families moved into the area seeking affordable housing and "good" schools.

Adobe Viejo Unified School District has grown rapidly in the past two decades. The public school system incorporates wide ethnic and economic diversity, but it has confronted the typical urban problems of violence, crime, and infrastructure decay later than most districts its size. Until the 1970s, the majority of Adobe Viejo's students were Anglo, from middle- and working-class households. Waves of immigration from Southeast Asia, and increases in the number of families moving from Mexico had begun to transform the complexion of Adobe Viejo's student population by the late 1970s.

Today, with its clear priorities for instruction and appetite for reform, Adobe Viejo epitomizes a "moving" district. It has established a national reputation as an innovative school system, and teachers rate Adobe Viejo as a good place to work. District support for teachers' involvement in professional organizations and participation in professional activities on state and national levels has fostered a lively sense of professionalism among district teachers and generally positive teacher-district relations. These positive relationships have enabled the district to weather the consequences of severe budget shortfalls and yearly deep cuts in the operating program better than other California districts, such as Mostaza, similarly challenged by declining support from the state (the legacy of Proposition 13). Although the union and the district have experienced their share of tense negotiations, they have had little of the bitterness and hostility that characterized relations in Mostaza. The three public high schools we studied in Adobe Viejo—Valley, Onyx Ridge, and

Ibsen—are about the same size (around 1,200 students) but differ considerably in terms of student population and mission.

Valley High School. Valley High School talks about itself as a "leftover school." Valley, once "one of the big schools, one of the best in [Adobe Viejo]," has confronted changes in its student population similar to those at Rancho and Esperanza in Mostaza. Demographic shifts and district desegregation plans have changed Valley's student body from predominately middle class to a student population of approximately 60 percent minority—Latinos and students from Pacific Rim countries who travelacross Adobe Viejo. These students, whose low-income status qualifies the school for federal Title 1 resources, occupy the seats formerly filled by students from the area's middle-class families, "creamed off" when a new high school, Onyx Ridge, was built to the north. Many Valley faculty members speak of their current students in disparaging terms and the teacher community ethos is sour and dispirited. The physical condition of the school exacerbates these feelings: The physical plant is run down, texts are frayed, and equipment is dated. The heavily enrolled business class, for example, still worked away on manual typewriters as late as 1990.

Onyx Ridge. Onyx Ridge, from the day its doors opened in the early 1980s, has been perceived by teachers and the Adobe Viejo community as one of the "best" comprehensive secondary schools in the district. Onyx Ridge's community is predominantly upper middle class and white; the approximately 250 students bused in as part of the district voluntary desegregation program are relatively invisible, concentrated in basic or remedial classes. The student body at Onyx Ridge generally is academically successful. Over one quarter test at the state-defined gifted level; more than 80 percent go directly to college. Teachers comment on the high levels of motivation and "conscientious work habits" exhibited by their college-bound students. Teachers and administrators describe Onyx Ridge parents, many of whom are professors at a nearby university or professionals in Adobe Viejo's active financial sector, as highly demanding and "an active force in the school." Teachers consider Onyx Ridge the school they would like to retire from. "Once they get here they don't leave. . . . This is it." There are "more amenities"; it's more "high tech"; it's quieter and nicer physically. Teachers talk about the administration as highly supportive, and about each other as "professionals" and the "crème de la crème."

Ibsen. Ibsen, a performing arts magnet located in a poor African-American neighborhood across town from Valley and Onyx Ridge, was founded in 1977 as part of the district's desegregation plan. Ibsen draws about half of its diverse student population from the neighborhood and the rest travel from twenty-two different attendance areas throughout the district. Approximately half of the students are European American, more than one-third are African American, and the other students come from Mexican, Filipino, or Pacific Rim backgrounds. Ibsen does not select students on the basis of talent. Admission turns on "a complex set of variables," including race, location, grade level, and whether a sibling goes to Ibsen. Students hoping for a spot at the school make up a long waiting list.

Ibsen students successfully manage heavy performing arts and academic requirements, and almost 90 percent go on to higher education. Balancing arts and academics constitutes an ongoing struggle for Ibsen faculty. Teachers of academic subjects often feel they take second place to the demands of the arts schedule, and they feel a loss of prestige among subject-area colleagues for not being a "real" teacher in a "real" school. The school's influential principal insists on a personalized, student-centered school environment, and has instituted policies, such as a faculty advisory structure, to promote student success.

Oak Valley School District

Oak Valley, located to the north of Adobe Viejo, used to serve a semirural and relatively affluent suburb. Oak Valley has also experienced great change in the past two decades, but change of a very different sort than Adobe Viejo. A "country bumpkin sort of town" in the mid-1960s, the district had grown almost tenfold by the mid-1980s as commuters from Adobe Viejo moved north to enjoy a more rural setting and peaceful neighborhoods. Downtown Oak Valley still has a small-town feel, but new hotels and high-rise apartments popping up along the freeway have reconfigured the landscape. Cow pastures are turned into housing developments on a monthly basis, and stark new neighborhoods await the growth of recently planted landscaping to soften the scene.

The district's history also has been one of steady growth and steady progress in terms of the professional quality of its schools and teachers. The new building and rising affluence have provided a financial cushion to buffer the district from the general turbulence of post–Proposition 13 school finance. The district has been able to equip its new schools adequately and to provide generous support for teachers' professional activities. Expectations have been clear: Oak Valley teachers will be up-to-date and the best. Oak Valley has gained a national reputation for innovation and excellence, for decentralization of many decision areas to schools and teachers, and for innovative policies such as a peer assessment program for teachers. Oak Valley has had its share of tension with the teachers' organization as contracts are renegotiated, but even in the midst of prickly union-district discussions, Oak Valley received praise from teachers as "the best district around," a "destination district" in career terms. Pride of profession infuses Oak Valley district.

Oak Valley High School. Oak Valley High School describes itself as the "archetypal comprehensive high school." The school opened in 1968; its student population had grown from 600 to more than 3,000 by 1990. This rapid growth led to changes in the use of facilities, such as the loss of any common room, the need for teachers to share classrooms, and the strong departmentalization of the faculty. Oak Valley's faculty is relatively young, "very professional, very caring for students and for each other." Selection to the Oak Valley faculty has been considered a professional compliment of the highest order. "I thought I'd died and gone to heaven," the principal recalled.

Most of Oak Valley's students are college bound; those who do not plan to go to college right away look forward to enrolling in a training program associated with one of the nearby industrial or commercial concerns. Teachers express pride in their students and the community. One teacher called the school a "wonderful little circle," because it attracts good students, good teachers, and enjoys strong community support. Oak Valley's student body is relatively homogeneous, comprising mostly

European-American youth from comfortable circumstances. "The students are really a cut above," say their teachers.

MICHIGAN DISTRICTS AND SCHOOLS

Our Michigan sample includes four districts—two urban districts and their adjacent suburban districts. These districts have confronted economic pressures as have the California districts, but the squeeze has come from a different source. Whereas California district budgets reflect the state of the California economy as a whole and local revenue limits established under the 1978 Proposition 13, Michigan districts are responsible for the bulk of their own financial support. Michigan educators have relied on local voters to respond to budget shortfalls and finance the schools at an adequate level. The local economies of three of the four districts we studied have drastically declined, and voter hesitation to approve new funds for their schools has demoralized teachers. Michigan districts also have greater instructional authority than do California districts, and offer interesting contrast on that point.

Burton School District

The Burton metropolitan area is dominated physically and economically by two aging industrial facilities. Plants that once ran round the clock and employed most of Burton's white- and blue-collar workforce now sit silent. Burton was emblematic of the American dream in the first seventy-five years of the twentieth century; at century's close it epitomizes the economic downtrend that has ravaged urban America. "For Sale" signs, deserted buildings, and eviction notices appear in all of Burton's neighborhoods, from the proud Victorian houses of Burton's professionals to the aging apartments and multifamily dwellings of the working class and poor. The shops and enterprises that supplied and supported these industries struggle to survive or are shuttered closed. Burton's population is approximately 50 percent Anglo and 50 percent minority. Waves of immigrants from central Europe made up Burton's ethnic minority working class for the first half of the century; now Burton's minority citizens are predominately African American.

The Burton district has struggled to maintain the public schools in a climate of fiscal crisis and social disintegration. As recession washed over the local economy in the 1980s, teachers experienced massive layoffs; faculty learned to keep track of their seniority in terms of months and days. Teachers have thus seen the Burton district less as a bureaucratic arrangement than as a system of support personified by visiting district coordinators and directors. District guidelines and curricula have been provided to the schools, where teachers interpret them as they see fit. District officials have taken an active role in helping Burton teachers manage shortfalls, missing or broken materials, and locating resources. The Burton teachers' union has good relationships with the district and has worked with officials to respond to budget issues. Both of the Burton high schools in our sample still struggle with eroding resources for the school and the growing poverty among their school community.

Highlander. Highlander has always served the children of Burton's low-income, blue-collar families, but conditions for those families and children worsened dramatically in the 1980s as jobs and social services became scarce. It enrolls a "majority minority" African-American student population and since its founding has considered itself an "underdog" school because of the low-income status of its clientele. Highlander faculty express pride in their school, defending the institution and the students. Highlander students experience violence at home and on the streets; drugs, pregnancy, crime are everyday considerations. High rates of student absenteeism, tardiness, and transiency challenge Highlander teachers continually. Highlander teachers have responded by broadening their role to include nonacademic interactions, and teachers routinely "lend a hand" to colleagues short of materials or funds. "Family" is a metaphor used often to describe the Highlander school community.

Washington Academy. Washington Academy, the antithesis of Highlander's close and supportive community, issued from a shotgun marriage between two very different Burton secondary schools. The very traditional Burton Academy committed to fundamentalist religious values, strict discipline, and codes of behavior was superimposed on Washington High School, a "failing" inner-city high school. Students apply for admission; Washington Academy, a school of choice, is "recommended for students who do best under firm direction and adult guidance." The student body is racially balanced (approximately half African American, half European American); student socioeconomic status ranges from extreme poverty to moderate privilege, although most students enjoy very modest family means. In contrast to Highlander's more student-centered practices, teaching at Washington Academy and expectations for students' learning derive from "back to basics" approaches.

Dover School District

Dover is an affluent, Anglo suburb of approximately 6,000 that is located at the edge of Burton, yet it feels a thousand miles away. The Dover community has been home to many of the executives who run Burton's industries and other "old money" families who have long lived in that part of the state. The district serves the entire township, with a population of more than 23,000. Dover High School's faculty and parents mirror pride in place and students. Even though a growing number of new students, both European-American and African-American children of blue-collar workers living in a nearby trailer park or housing project, have entered Dover High School, the "typical" Dover student remains middle or upper-middle class, European American, high achieving, and college bound. "Virtually all of my students want to go to college," said a Dover High School teacher. "For them, failure is a B." Parental pressure for student success was constant consideration in teachers' work lives.

Dover High School. Dover High School has a reputation for high academic standards and teacher professionalism. Its faculty are expected to pursue their professional growth as a top priority. District administrators have adopted a decentralized, shared-decision-making model of management, involving teachers in all aspects of decisions affecting curriculum, school organization, and instructional policies. Students and parents, too, are given a voice in district-level decisions and take an active role in district governance. An issue for Dover is the changing nature of the district's student population. Dover's reputation for excellence was established years ago, when the community was essentially middle and upper class. Some educators worry that the district is "living in the past" as it plans, rather than considering how it can meet the needs of new, nontraditional students.

Falls Park School District

Falls Park, one of Michigan's larger urban centers located in a politically conservative area of the state, shares Burton's economic woes. Its economy and neighborhoods date back to the era of stagecoaches, when Falls Park was a stop on the westbound line. Old Victorians from the early 1800s share central city space with new high-rise office buildings. Falls Park's economy, which centers on light manufacturing, has eroded as longtime businesses have closed their plants. For years a quietly prosperous city, Falls Park today confronts economic distress in all areas of public services, most centrally education.

Our study schools in this region include two public schools in the central city district and a public alternative school in an adjacent suburban district. Apart from its sector and the social background of its students, the alternative school is comparable in mission to the Greenfield independent school in the Mostaza region of California.

The district's school population is approximately 50 percent Anglo and 50 percent ethnic minority, predominately African Americans whose families have lived in the area for generations. Approximately 50 percent of the students come from economically disadvantaged homes, and most of those youngsters are minority. The district goes to the public each year with millage proposals to raise funds to support the schools. Difficulty in passing these proposals has resulted in annual layoffs and recalls of district personnel. In the last year of this study, all teachers with less than twenty-three years' seniority were laid off and not recalled until a second millage vote passed. Few teachers start the year in Falls Park knowing what they will be teaching, or to whom. Despite this fiscal and organizational chaos, the district struggles to keep its reputation as an educational leader. With grants from local businesses, the district has carried out an extensive professional development program for teachers in workshops after school or in summer institutes. Despite severe budget crises, union-district relations have been amicable. In contrast to Burton, which leaves many decisions about instruction up to teachers, Falls Park takes a fairly heavy-handed role in determining what is taught in district schools. "The district leads you down the straight and narrow," said a teacher. Both of the Falls Park high schools included in this study—LaSalle and Monroe—struggle as well to maintain proud reputations of the past, and to meet the needs of their changing student bodies.

LaSalle High School. LaSalle High School prides itself on its professional orientation and reputation for academic excellence, and indeed for many years it has been perceived as "the best in the district." Faculty here have confronted changes in the student body similar to most urban secondary schools. LaSalle's clientele has changed from a relatively homogeneous, European-American, middle- and upper-class, college-bound population to a diverse student body of all income levels. European Americans make up approximately 56 percent of the student body; African Americans, 40 percent; and there is a small number of Asian and Hispanic students.

More than half of LaSalle's experienced faculty remember the "good old days" of highly motivated, academically talented students and find it difficult to adapt to the students who come to school today. The school has responded to diversity in student preparation and academic competencies by creating two tracks, regular and advanced. Advanced classes are strongly subject focused, teacher dominated, and aimed at "those who do very well." Students thus figure either as constraints or rewards at LaSalle. Teachers comment that students in their "terminal classes" bring little satisfaction. Nevertheless, LaSalle teachers generally are proud of their school and its traditions. The principal is seen as supportive and important to the schools' reputation as a good place to work.

Monroe High School. Monroe High School across town differs from LaSalle only by degree. Monroe's student population is approximately half European American and half African American: "two schools in one building," teachers said. Monroe serves more extremely poor and transient students than does LaSalle. Like LaSalle's faculty, teachers at Monroe remember the "old days," "the students we used to have," and the school's traditions of academic excellence and leadership. Faculty morale has plummeted with changes in the student body. Teachers have rated the performance of approximately 50 percent of their students as "unsatisfactory." Monroe faculty, like their colleagues at LaSalle, see few students in the middle: "We have a top and a bottom."

Oneida School District

Oneida, a small- to medium-size suburban school district that enrolls approximately 6,000 students, serves mostly as a bedroom community for the city of Falls Park. Unlike the prosperous Dover outside Burton, this district is predominantly lower middle class, with some middle-class parents. There are a number of housing projects in the district, which are home to most of the district's extremely poor families. Oneida, as financially strapped as most Michigan districts, has had to pink slip teachers for the past several years when budgets could not be balanced and millage efforts failed. Teachers worried about their jobs not only in terms of seniority, but also in terms of being "bumped" by a more senior colleague and reassigned to another position. However, the community supports its schools financially as well as it can; a 1992 bond brought much additional funding for technology.

The district's central office is small, with only three administrators, a superintendent, and two assistants. All three have been with the district for more than ten years. The teacher population also is stable, most teachers having worked in the district for ten years or more. The Oneida teachers' union is strong and works very closely with central administration to maintain good union-management relations. Oneida's teachers and administrators are very loyal to their district, the buildings in which they work, and the community they serve.

Prospect. Prospect, the Oneida school we studied, has a similar feel and mission to Greenfield, a California independent school. Both are small alternative high schools. Prospect, founded in 1979, provides an interesting contrast to Greenfield, however, because its class size is much larger, and its teachers are assigned by the district personnel office. There is a great range of ability in the school, but "basically all of our kids [come] from situations were they were outcasts, for one reason or another." The student population fluctuates at the beginning of term and decreases as students drop out as the term progresses. The school promotes a comfortable, family atmosphere and provides broad support for students through personal relationships and advising groups. Students are "treated as adults," and they play a central role in the way the school is run. But parent involvement and interest in their students' education is low. Teachers mentioned: "I'll call up their parents and they'll say, 'Well, I've given up on them.'" Teachers take up this parenting and support role. Collegiality among the staff is extremely high and shared effort assumed. "I don't think any one of us would be able to teach in this job without the rest of the staff." The school's principal is key to the character and strength of the school. As a signal of commitment to a student-centered environment, he greets each student by name at the door every morning.

➤➤➤

Our primary goal in constructing a sample for this study was to be able to capture diverse combinations of embedded system and community contexts of teaching. The contrasts represented in our sample enable us to look at a range of embedded school contexts, while also comparing schools with others in the same state and district contexts.

Teacher Survey Data

We conducted schoolwide teacher surveys in all sixteen schools in our sample in 1989, 1990, and 1991. Data from the 1991 survey are used in analyses reported here. The teacher respondent N for this survey year was 623, representing a response rate of 74 percent for the pooled faculty population and an average of 77 percent for the sample schools. Some analyses, such as those focused on district contexts, use data for public school teachers only ($N = 538$); analyses of subject departments use data for math, English, science, and social studies teachers in comprehensive high schools ($N = 238$).

Survey scales were developed to represent coherent patterns in teachers' responses to a set of similar survey items. We used principal components analysis to identify particular items that define a common factor and added the items together to form a scale. Teacher scores on a scale were then standardized, using the mean and standard deviation for the population (for those scales that replicate national survey scales, such as "collegiality," we standardize teacher scores using national norms). We report data in standard scores to facilitate comparison across cases; in general, we treat a difference of .5 or more standard deviation units as meaningful. Depending upon the unit of analysis, we aggregate teachers' standard scores on a scale to form a mean for a subject area, a subject department, a school, or a district.

SURVEY SCALES

Survey scales and component items are listed below, according to the chapter in which they are first discussed in text or endnote. For each scale, we show the wording of component items, and their stem question, as they appeared in the 1991 Teacher Questionnaire. Alpha coefficients are reported to indicate the scale's internal consistency, or the degree of coherence among items that compose the scale.

CHAPTER 3

Collegiality (5 items; alpha = .84)
Using the scale provided, please indicate the extent to which you agree or disagree with each of the following statements:

    a. You can count on most staff members to help out anywhere, anytime even though it may not be part of their official assignment.

    b. Teachers in this school are continually learning and seeking new ideas.

    c. There is a great deal of cooperative effort among staff members.

    d. Staff members maintain high standards.

    e. This school seems like a big family, everyone is so close and cordial.

Technical Culture (6 items; alpha = .73)
To what extent does each of the following statements describe relationships among each of the teachers *in your primary subject area* in this school?

    a. We have very different ideas about what we should emphasize in the curriculum (reverse coded).

    b. We have little idea of each other's teaching goals and classroom practices (reverse coded).

    c. There is little disagreement about what should be taught in our subject area.

d. There is a lot of disagreement among us about how to teach the subject (reverse coded).

e. We share views of students and how to relate to them.

Expectations for Student Achievement (6 items; alpha = .60)

On the scale below, indicate how much you agree or disagree with each of the following statements:

a. No matter how hard I try, some students will not be able to learn aspects of my subject matter (reverse coded).

b. My expectations about how much students should learn are not as high as they used to be (reverse coded).

c. Students who work hard and do well deserve more of my time than those who do not (reverse coded).

d. There is really very little I can do to ensure that most of my students achieve at a high level (reverse coded).

e. The attitudes and habits students bring to my classes greatly reduce their chances for academic success (reverse coded).

g. Most of the students I teach are not capable of learning material I should be teaching them (reverse coded).

Student Decline (7 items; alpha = .77)

Indicate how much you agree or disagree with each of these statements about students in your classes this year.

a. Students in my classes today are less prepared than students I have taught in previous years.

b. My students are as able and motivated as students I have taught in the past (reverse coded).

c. The attitudes and habits students bring to my classes greatly reduce their chances for academic success.

d. Students in my classes today are better prepared than students I have taught in previous years (reverse coded).

e. Most of the students I teach are not capable of learning the material I should be teaching them.

f. My current students care more about education than most students I taught in the past (reverse coded).

g. Students in my classes today have more serious social and family problems than students I have taught in previous years.

Bureaucratic Constraints (6 items; alpha = .76)

Using the scale provided, please indicate the extent to which you agree or disagree with each of the following statements:

a. Those assigned to evaluate my teaching have a good understanding of my course content and instructional approach (reverse coded).

b. I have to follow rules at this school that conflict with my best professional judgment.

c. I have to buck rules in order to do what I think needs to be done for my students.

d. Too often decisions are made by building staff are ignored or reversed by central office administrators.

e. I can take little action at this school until a superior approves it.

f. The rules and regulations at this school don't make my job any easier.

Static Subject (3 items; alpha = .61)

For your most frequently taught subject area, please indicate the extent to which you agree or disagree with the following statements.

a. Thinking creatively is an important part of the subject matter I teach (reverse coded).

b. Knowledge in my subject area is always changing (reverse coded).

c. The subject I teach is rather cut and dried.

Routine Work (5 items; alpha = .83)

To what extent do you agree or disagree with the following statements about your day-to-day job in this school (consider your work outside, as well as inside, the classroom).

a. Many of my work tasks are the same from day to day.

b. I rely on established procedures and practices in my job.

c. My work is basically routine.

d. My work activities vary considerably from day to day (reverse coded).

e. My job duties are quite repetitious.

Personalization (4 items; alpha = .57)

The statements below concern goals for educational outcomes

and for relationships with students. Please indicate how strongly you agree or disagree with each statement as it applies to your own teaching philosophy and practice.

    a. I try very hard to show my students that I care about them.

    b. It is important for me to know something about my students' families.

    c. I feel that I should be accessible to students even if it means meeting with them before or after school, during my prep or free period, etc.

    d. I believe that teachers should keep their relationships with students in classes focused strictly on coursework (reverse coded).

CHAPTER 4

Teacher Learning Community (8 items; alpha = .85)
Please indicate how strongly you agree or disagree with each of the following statements regarding your current feelings about teaching in general and your present job.

    a. I feel that I have many opportunities to learn new things in my present job.

    b. I feel supported by colleagues to try out new ideas.

Using the scale provided, please indicate the extent to which you agree or disagree with each of the following statements about working conditions in your school.

    c. In this school we solve problems we don't just talk about them.

    d. My job provides me continuing professional stimulation and growth.

    e. The staff seldom evaluates its programs and activities (reverse coded).

    f. In this school, I am encouraged to experiment with my teaching.

    g. Teachers in this school are constantly learning and seeking new ideas.

    h. The principal is interested in innovations and new ideas.

Job Satisfaction (2 items; alpha = .73)
How much of the time do you feel satisfied with your job in this

school? (4 point scale: almost never, some of the time, most of the time, all of the time.)

Using the scale provided, please indicate the extent to which you agree or disagree with [the following statement]:

    a. I usually look forward to each working day at this school.

Commitment to Teaching Career (2 items; alpha = .52)
Please indicate how strongly you agree or disagree with each of the following statements regarding your current feelings about teaching in general and your present job.

    a. If I could get a higher paying job, I'd leave teaching in a minute (reverse coded).

    b. I feel little loyalty to the teaching profession (reverse coded).

Professional Engagement (5 items; alpha = .71)
Please indicate how strongly you agree or disagree with each of the following statements regarding your current feelings about teaching in general and your present job.

    a. I am willing to put in a great deal of effort beyond that usually expected of others.

    b. I feel that I am improving each year as a teacher.

    c. I don't seem to have as much enthusiasm now as I did when I began teaching (reverse coded).

    d. I really love the subject I teach most frequently.

    e. I am always eager to hear about ways to improve my teaching.

Satisfaction with Courses and Students (2 items: range 2–14)
Please indicate on the scale below how strongly you feel, one way or the other, about specific conditions of your current teaching job.

    a. The courses I am assigned to teach.

    b. The students I am assigned to teach.

Satisfaction with Professional Support (5 items: range 5–35)
Please indicate on the scale below how strongly you feel, one way or the other, about specific conditions of your current teaching job.

a. Extent of support I receive from site administrators.
b. Extent of support I receive from school colleagues.
c. Opportunities to participate in decisions affecting my work.
d. Opportunities to collaborate with school colleagues.
e. Opportunities for professional development.

CHAPTER 5

Principal Leadership (9 items; alpha = .86)
Using the scale provided, please indicate the extent to which you agree or disagree with each of the following statements:

a. The principal does a poor job of getting resources for this school (reverse coded).
b. The principal deals effectively with pressures from outside the school that might interfere with my teaching.
c. The principal sets priorities, makes plans, and sees that they are carried out.
d. Goals and priorities for the school are clear.
e. Staff members are recognized for a job well done.
f. The principal knows what kind of school he/she wants and has communicated it to the staff.
g. The school's administration knows the problems faced by the staff.
h. The school administration's behavior toward the staff is supportive and encouraging.
i. The principal lets staff members know what is expected of them.

District Professionalism (6 items; alpha = .82)
Now indicate how strongly you agree or disagree with the statements regarding your feelings about the district in which you teach.

a. I would accept almost any class or school assignment in order to keep working for this district.
b. It would take very little change in my present circumstances to cause me to leave this district (reverse coded).

c. I feel that this district inspires the very best in the job performance of its teachers.

d. Often I find it difficult to agree with this district's policies on important matters relating to its teachers (reverse coded).

e. I am proud to tell others that I work for this district.

f. The district is a source of considerable dissatisfaction with my teaching job (reverse coded).

NOTES

Chapter One

1. On professionalizing strategies, see, for example, Shedd and Bacharach 1991; Darling-Hammond and Berry 1988; Furhman and O'Day 1996. Smith and O'Day (1991) describe the principles of so-called systemic reform and the ways in which diverse policy tools could be aligned to support reform throughout the system.

2. Cusick 1973; Metz 1978; Yee 1990; Eckert 1989; Lortie 1975; Huberman 1993; Jackson 1968.

3. For example, Bruckerhoff 1991; McPherson 1972; Natkins 1986; and Nehring 1989 provide compelling accounts of teachers' everyday work lives.

4. Grossman and Stodolsky 1994, 1995; Stodolsky and Grossman, 1996, 1992; Stodolsky 1988; Ball and Goodson 1984; Goodson 1983; Siskin 1994; Siskin and Little 1995.

5. By century's end, a movement to counter state authority over education standards and accountability was underway. Because the new professional standards challenge conventional wisdom—taken-for-granted standards of good teaching—their adoption by some states and districts has engendered considerable controversy. On one hand, upholders of traditional education within and outside the profession contest the scientific grounding of the standards; on the other hand, proponents of education equity contest the use of standards in accountability systems when poor and immigrant students are disadvantaged by their prior education resources.

6. The sense we make of the diverse California and Michigan high school professional communities has evolved since our earlier publications in the 1990s, which documented boundaries of teacher communities and conditions at department, school, and district levels that shaped teachers' professional beliefs and attitudes (McLaughlin and Talbert 1993; Talbert

and McLaughlin 1994). As we grappled with puzzles and problems of teacher community, through sustained analysis of these data and subsequent research on high school reform, new ways of seeing and understanding high school professional communities evolved.

Chapter Two

1. This quote and the case study from which it derives can be found in *Adolescent Worlds* by Patricia Phelan, Ann Davidson, and Hanh Yu (1998, 24). Phelan, Davidson, and Yu carried out the "Students' Multiple Worlds" study in four California schools in our sample as part of the CRC's larger research in secondary schools. Their research engaged students from diverse background in questions of their family, peer, and school worlds and the contexts that shaped them. The students included in this research were in the classrooms and schools of the high school teachers we feature in this study.

2. U.S. high school students work longer hours than teenagers in most other countries do. Researchers are divided on the effects of adolescent employment on grades, but agree that more than twenty hours a week at a job hurts both grades and health. Teens, even youth from advantaged homes, say they work primarily to have money for clothes, cars, and entertainment (Viadero 1998, 10).

3. Theodore Sizer uses a triangle to describe what he calls the "stuff" of teaching and learning. Joseph P. McDonald (1992) elaborates and sharpens this image with the term "wild triangle," which conveys the tempestuous, unpredictable, and intense character of the classroom core. David Hawkins also offers a triangle as representation of adults and children engaged together in "worthy subject-matter": I, Thou, and It. "Without a Thou," writes Hawkins, "there is no I evolving. Without an It, there is no content for the context, no figure and no heat, but only an affair of mirrors confronting each other" (1974, 49, 52).

4. These distinctions among teachers' responses to challenges to instructional tradition are similar to the three patterns of adaptation Lacey (1977) identified for beginning teachers: (1) strategic compliance; (2) internalized adjustment; (3) strategic redefinition of the situation.

5. Susan Rosenholtz uses the term "certainty" to refer to teachers' instructional decision making and beliefs about "how teaching should best be done in ways that enable their student charges to learn and grow" (1989, 4). Certainty focused on routines of practice, however, is likely to constrain student learning opportunities and generate high failure rates in classes serving nontraditional students.

6. See Grossman and Stodolsky 1993 for elaboration of this case example.

7. Ann Locke Davidson's ethnographic study (1996) of students in a subsample of schools participating in CRC research elaborates the diverse educational settings nontraditional students encountered as they moved through their school day.

8. Ann Locke Davidson presents another analysis of these student data in her book *Making and Molding Identities in School.* This comment comes from her case analysis of Ryan Moore (1996, 151).

Chapter Three

1. We use Etienne Wenger's (1998) meanings of "community of practice." The concept focuses on the inherently social character of work in an occupation and organization, and on the particular shared goals and joint enterprises that work groups construct in the course of their daily work lives. Lave and Wagner (1991) explicate how social interaction with colleagues serves as an interpretive frame for practice and medium for learning (for an application in mathematics teaching, see also Lave 1991 and Stein, Silver, and Smith 1998). Because the concept assumes a social practice, or shared enterprise, high school professional communities with weak collegial ties and strong privacy norms of practice fall beyond its analytic scope.

2. Leslie Santee Siskin (1994) provides an intensive analysis of academic departments in three CRC schools; Little (1993) compares academic and vocational departments in several schools in this study. Siskin and Little (1995) offer a collection of essays on the topic of departmental organization and the high school.

3. We analyzed variance in teachers' scores on a "technical culture" survey scale and found that 31 percent of the variance was between departments, with only 4 percent between subject areas and less between schools. A measure of expectations for student achievement showed a similar pattern: 21 percent of the variance was between departments, compared with 7 percent between schools and none between subjects. For more detail see Talbert and McLaughlin (1994, 136–38).

4. Their department means on the technical culture survey scale differ by nearly 1.5 standard deviations (.48 and −.97, respectively, in relation to norms for the whole study sample).

5. Survey measures capture some of the cultural differences that shape teaching and learning in these two high school departments. On average, the Oak Valley English department differs by nearly 1 standard deviation from social studies teachers on the "student decline" scale and .75 standard deviation on a "routine work" scale (five-item scale).

6. On a survey scale measuring teachers' perceptions of bureaucratic constraints on their work, the social studies teachers averaged .75 standard deviation above the English teachers.

7. We compared English, math, social studies, and science teachers' scores on survey measures of "static" (versus dynamic) subject (three-item scale) and "routine work." The sample sizes for each subject were 109, 82, 85, and 81, respectively. Math teachers averaged significantly higher on both scales; English teachers scored lowest, though not significantly below science and social studies teachers. The difference between

math and English teachers' ratings of their subject as static is nearly 1.5 standard deviations (using the distribution for teachers of all four subjects combined).

8. These math departments differ significantly on survey measures of teachers' conceptions of their students, subject, and teaching role. Differences in department averages are .75 standard deviation for student decline, static subject, and routine work. The departments differ by more than 1.5 standard deviation on a measure of "personalization," or teachers' inclinations to get to know their students as individuals.

9. The distinction between knowledge *of* practice and knowledge *for* practice is one made by Marilyn Cochran-Smith and Susan Lytle (1998). The knowledge *for* practice is the sort of subject expertise, learned through formal course work and the like, that traditional communities of practice prize; the knowledge *of* practice is the kind of situated knowledge that teacher learning communities develop through collective inquiry into their practice.

Chapter Four

1. Merit pay schemes have a spotty and transient history across U.S. school districts, and the National Board for Professional Teaching Standards' system for certifying exemplary teachers has thus far involved a minute percentage of teachers (about 9,000 out of roughly 3 million teachers had applied for board certification as of early 2000).

2. National survey data from the Schools and Staffing Survey for 1990–91 indicate that, at the time of our study, out-of-field teaching in public high schools across the nation ranged from 17 percent for science and social studies to 31 percent for mathematics (Ingersoll 1999, fig. 2).

3. Our survey data show that teachers in typical high schools who teach classes in different tracks over the course of a day feel more successful in their higher-track classes (Rowan, Raudenbush, and Kang 1991); their sense of efficacy and professional rewards vary according to the students they teach.

4. The tendency to judge an individual's status within an occupation by the social status of his or her clientele may be rather common. A study of the social system of Chicago lawyers (Heinz 1982) observed that lawyers derive professional status from their clients' socioeconomic status and, in the absence of overriding professional rewards, experience their careers in terms of such external markers.

5. Teachers classified as "low track" reported teaching only "remedial" or "general" classes on our survey; teachers classified as "high track" were teaching at least two "honors" or AP classes and otherwise only "academic" classes. Across the twelve comprehensive public schools in our sample, teacher tracking varies considerably between subject departments within schools and between schools in a particular subject. In each of the four core academic subjects, we observed at least one department/school

in which there were no low-track or high-track teachers, and at least one department in which nearly half of all teachers were tracked into high-level or low-level classes (the upper end ranged from 40 percent for social studies to 50 percent for English). Those departments with high levels of teacher tracking were the communities most heavily invested in traditional practice. Interestingly, the extent of course tracking varied less across departments, revealing that teacher tracking mainly reflects differences in teacher assignment policies, rather than variation in high school curriculum structures.

6. National survey data show this broad phenomenon across U.S. schools. Schools with the highest proportions of poor students and students of color have the least well prepared teachers (Darling-Hammond 1997; Ferguson 1991).

7. Across all sixteen high schools in our sample, teachers' ratings of their workplace on a "teacher learning community" survey scale (see appendix C for items that compose the scale) correlated highly with measures of several career outcomes: job satisfaction ($r = .57$), professional engagement ($.51$), and commitment to a teaching career ($.41$).

8. We found significant department differences in teachers' survey responses to questions concerning job satisfaction and engagement. Oak Valley English teachers score 1 standard deviation higher than their social studies colleagues on a survey scale measuring satisfaction with professional support, .5 standard deviations higher on satisfaction with courses and students, and .75 standard deviations higher on professional engagement. The department means were computed using the mean and standard deviation of all Oak Valley teachers' scores on each of the survey scales.

9. The difference of nearly 1.5 standard deviations indicates that there is very little overlap between even the highest ratings among Rancho math teachers and the lowest ratings among the Esperanza math teachers.

10. Across the comprehensive high schools in our sample, the percentage of math teachers with at least a bachelor's degree in mathematics ranged from 40 percent in Ibsen to 100 percent in Dover. In each of the Mostaza district math departments, only 50 percent of the faculty had this level of subject preparation. In general, math teachers in Michigan high schools had stronger subject backgrounds; in three, more than 80 percent of the faculty had a B.A. or higher in mathematics, while the highest level among the California math departments was 75 percent for Onyx Ridge.

11. We computed rotation rates using three years of math departments' master schedules that showed individual teachers' course assignments. A rotation was counted when a teacher taught a particular course in year 2 but not in year 1, or in year 3 but not in year 2. An average rate of course rotation was computed for each teacher and then standardized using the mean and standard deviation for all math teachers. The average rotation rate for Esperanza was 2 standard deviations above that for Rancho's math department.

12. Teachers' survey ratings on the "satisfaction with professional support" scale range from 1.3 (Ibsen) to 2.5 (Prospect) standard deviations higher than the public school mean for our sample; on the "satisfaction with courses and students" scale, these schools' means range from .5 (Ibsen and Greenfield) to 1.4 (Prospect) standard deviations higher. "Professional engagement" scores range from .5 (Ibsen) to .9 (Prospect) standard deviation units above the public school norm.

Chapter Five

1. Leslie Siskin's 1994 book, *Realms of Knowledge: Academic Departments in Secondary Schools,* provides a rich analysis of academic departments in three of the high schools in our sixteen-school study, including Oak Valley and Rancho. Siskin's research builds upon research traditions concerned with the social organization of schools and with subject-matter disciplines.

2. This analysis of variance in teacher scores on the teacher learning community (TLC) scale assessed (1) how much variance is explained by differences in teachers' mean scores across all academic departments in our public high schools (28 percent); (2) how much variance is explained by differences between the schools (13 percent); and (3) how much variance is explained by differences between academic subjects (3 percent). The amount of variance in teachers' TLC scores that can be attributed uniquely to differences in department communities within schools is 12 percent (28–13–3 percent). To estimate variance associated with each organization level, we represented all units at each level with dummy variables and used ordinary least-squares regression analysis to estimate variance explained by differences in means on the scale between them. Using the same technique with data for the full teacher sample, we estimated the unique variance in TLC that can attributed to each of the higher levels of our embedded sample: 6 percent for sector (independent versus public schools), 1 percent for state, and 4 percent for district within the public school sector. About half of the between-school variance is the difference between public and independent schools in our sample (6 percent between sectors, versus 13 percent between all schools).

3. In relation to national norms, the principals in our sample received ratings from their faculty that range from .5 standard deviation below the mean to over 3 standard deviations above the mean ratings for U.S. public high school principals. Our sample underrepresents high schools with very weak principals. Indeed, principals in nine of the sixteen schools receive teacher ratings on leadership that exceed 1 standard deviation above the national mean; this includes all three private schools, two public schools in Michigan, and four in California. Still, we have considerable variation in principal leadership across the schools in our sample. For example, within the Adobe Viejo district, Valley High School's principal received teacher ratings that average 3.1 standard deviations below those of Ibsen's principal.

4. For exceptions, see Murphy and Hallinger 1988; Spillane 1996; Spillane and Thompson 1997.

5. Note that teachers' ratings of Mostaza and Oak Valley describe almost non-overlapping distributions. These scores are district means of teachers' scores on the "district professionalism" scale (see appendix C); each teacher's score was first standardized using the overall mean and standard deviation for public school teachers in our sample.

6. As another example of focus on the district community, the district's dropout problem was defined as a concern for the system, not just for individual schools. The assistant superintendent told us that "every manager in the district—*everyone,* including central office staff, not just principals—has to do something with dropouts. This is included in their evaluations. We don't feel it is appropriate to say it is just a school site problem."

7. Relations between district administration and the teachers' union are part of the fabric of each district's professional community. Depending upon the quality of district professional community, the union plays a role ranging from adversarial in Mostaza to collaborative in Oak Valley. Comparing teacher communities in Rancho, Onyx Ridge, and Oak Valley, Nina Bascia (1994) found that the union occupies a much more prominent place in Mostaza's professional culture than it does in the cultures of other districts, where teachers' identification with the union depends more on personal values and histories.

8. An interesting and important exception to this general statement is found in English teachers' assessment of the district, which was higher than that of their colleagues. We understand this as a response to the district's very effective English resource person, who in some important ways came to represent "district" for the English teachers.

9. Educational researchers have largely ignored the relationships between state and local education agencies. An exception is James Spillane and Charles Thompson's (1997) study of interactions between state policy and features of a district. Most important to our question here, Spillane and Thompson found that "the most successful LEAs [local education authorities] were those in which educators had devoted a great deal of time to figuring out what state policies and ideas from professional sources might mean for instruction [and] they viewed time for reform chiefly in terms of what it would take for teachers and others to understand the reforms" (1997, 197).

10. These data are drawn from the National Center for Education Statistics *Common Core of Data: School Years 1988–89 through 1993-94* (NCES 1996, 96–316).

11. Cohen and Hill (1998) provide evidence that intensive professional development focused on math education standards has an impact on teachers' beliefs and practices and on their students' performance on state math assessments. Inverness Subject Area Network Studies document ways in which teachers' learning is supported within California's subject networks.

12. This is a brief summary of results from multivariate analyses of teacher survey data to assess context effects on professional outcomes. We used a series of ordinary least-squares (OLS) regression analyses, with two-staged regressions to capture the reciprocal relationship between teacher community and principal leadership, to estimate a parsimonious path model consistent with the correlation data. The path estimates and technical details for this analysis are available from the authors.

Chapter Six

1. Research on restructuring reforms in American schools supports our view that teachers' professional culture enacts structure, rather than the reverse. In a landmark national study of restructured schools, Fred Newmann and colleagues (1996) found that "authentic" instruction was not widespread in classrooms of restructured schools. The benefits for teaching of restructured schools—more planning time, interdependent work structures, school autonomy from regulatory constraints, and small size—depend on the character of the school's professional community. Not all communities use the "same" resources in the same ways to the same effect: inquiring school communities made good use of these structural tools to support authentic practice (1996, 287–90).

2. Talcott Parsons (1959) first wrote about the dual "socialization" and "selection" functions of elementary-secondary schooling. On one hand, schools are charged with promoting students' cognitive growth and development; on the other hand, they are meant to grade and rank students for unequal futures in society. These goals for education potentially compete and undermine teachers' commitment to providing students with equal learning opportunities.

3. This argument extends institutional theory of schooling to educational practice. Early theory and research argued that schools gain legitimacy and support by having administrative structures that are isomorphic with cultural norms of rational organization and "decoupled" from their instructional core (Meyer and Rowan 1977; Weick, 1976). We argue that high school teachers' work and local teaching cultures, while loosely controlled by administrative systems, are tightly coupled to norms of good education and desirable professional careers in the broader society.

4. Analysts of teaching have regarded cultural ideals for teaching as favoring individualism and undermining collaboration. Judith Warren Little (1982, 1990) considered the persistence of "privacy norms"; Susan Rosenholtz worried that teachers would not be "willing or prepared to surrender their classroom isolation for collaborative relations" (1989, 219); Michael Huberman (1990) imagined an ideal of "independent artisanship" as standing in the way of cohesive professional community.

5. During the late 1990s, in California at least, Peter Senge's *The Fifth Discipline: The Art and Practice of the Learning Organization* (1990) was

a staple in district professional development workshops, and teachers were widely exposed to principles of collaborative, innovative organization.

6. This was a theme in research on high schools in the early 1990s when school community was surfacing as an important force in teaching and when reformers found frustration in department resistance to join in whole-school reform.

7. For example, California's reform math frameworks and innovative programs such as the Interactive Mathematics Program (IMP) are the focus of the "math wars" that have raged on since the mid-1990s (see *Education Week,* 29 February 2000).

8. These competing cultural notions of standards for teaching and learning play out at the level of subject departments in high schools, as we documented for math departments in Rancho and Esperanza.

9. For extended discussion of the technical, normative, and political meanings and standards regarding equity in American education, see Oakes 1992.

10. Independent schools can manage this tension by forming charters in terms of their particular students' futures. In our sample, the independent schools' charters ranged from preparing students for top-tier colleges (Paloma) to ensuring a high school diploma (Greenfield).

11. For example, the National Science Foundation's State Systemic Initiative relied on state and local networks of teachers as a primary implementation strategy. California's SB 1274 provided supports for restructuring schools through networks and through discourse communities established to focus teachers on the challenges of changing school habits.

12. A social systems frame for education reform takes the promotion and support of teachers' learning communities both inside and outside of school as integral to their ability to respond successfully to pressures for change. Such a policy frame establishes increased occasions on site for professional dialogue and collaboration around teaching; sufficient time, space, and scale within schools to enable ongoing collegial exchange and collaboration; a rich menu of opportunities for learning that are connected to central facets and challenges of teaching in content.

13. Further, a national trend toward five-year programs that include a year-long school-based internship connected to education course work responds to research indicating that graduates of such programs are not only more successful but also more likely to remain in teaching than are graduates of traditional undergraduate teacher education programs (Ashton and Crocker 1987; also see Andrew 1990; Andrew and Schwab 1995). Currently, roughly 30 percent of beginning teachers leave teaching within the first five years; an internship phase of teacher education could significantly reduce this attrition rate.

14. Teachers who apply for board certification engage in an extended process of developing the examination portfolio of evidence of their professional practice within and outside the classroom. As of early 2000, the

NBPTS had certified almost five thousand teachers nationwide, with about a 40 percent pass rate over prior administrations of the performance assessment. More than nine thousand teachers have participated in the arduous examination process.

15. This initiative and related state or local efforts to establish hierarchy in teachers' careers carry messages that are likely to be interpreted differently according to the culture of high school professional communities. To the extent that the NBPTS credentialing movement legitimizes a hierarchical and competitive view of teaching competence, it will attract teachers in strong traditional high school communities and perhaps reinforce their culture. To the extent that it legitimizes and promotes teacher collaboration and innovation, teachers in strong learning communities will be attracted and gain authority for their leadership. Despite the situated meanings of such career initiatives, the content of NPBTS standards may move professional norms toward collaboration.

16. For a comprehensive summary of this scholarship, see the recent National Research Council publication *How People Learn* (Bransford, Brown, and Cocking 1999).

17. In Kentucky, California, Texas, and Vermont, 20–41 percent of all teachers participated in at least nine hours of professional development focused on subject matter, teaching methods, or student assessments (Darling-Hammond 1997, 34–35).

18. Anthony Bryk, Valerie Lee, and Peter Holland (1993) show that school professional community is a significant source of Catholic schools' relative success in educating poor urban youth. Brian Lord (1994) argues that "critical colleagueship" and professional community are central in teachers' efforts to meet the expectations set out in standards-based reforms. Mary Kay Stein, Edward Silver, and Margaret Smith (1998) and Rebecca Perry (1996) document ways in which teacher communities of practice support teachers' learning to reform their mathematics teaching. David Cohen and Heather Hill (2000) report significant positive gains on the CLAS exam in math for students whose teachers had been involved in sustained, intensive professional development focused on learning new ways of teaching mathematics.

19. Two current developments in American education fail to provide the necessary scope for teachers' collective authority and accountability over educational decisions. First, although site-based management structures typically include teacher representatives on councils responsible for making limited fiscal and schoolwide policy decisions, and although such arrangements may change teachers' sentiments about professional work outside the classroom, as Dan Lortie (1998) observed in studying teachers' responses to Chicago's local site management, their work and authority on these councils is only loosely connected to consequential decisions of curriculum and instruction and is decontextualized from the communities in which teachers work most closely. Second, because various state and

local accountability systems typically focus on student scores on standardized tests, they are not likely to establish conditions that prompt teachers to collaborate to change their practice. For one, the tests are developed elsewhere, thus removing from teacher communities primary authority and responsibility for assessing teaching and learning in their classes, departments, and schools. Often the content of such tests is misaligned with the educational goals, curriculum, and instruction of innovative teacher communities. Moreover, subcommunities of high school teaching are poorly represented in standardized testing programs, which tap only a few disciplines and often only selected grade levels. Such accountability systems are likely to undermine, rather than promote, collective authority and responsibility for core educational decisions in high school teacher communities.

Appendix A

1. In their original formulation of institutional theory on education organizations, Meyer and Rowan (1977) analyzed norms for rational organization as sources of school organization structure. Our use of institutional theory in analyzing teachers' work is concerned especially with norms for teaching practices in the environment of K–12 schooling. We focus on cultures and organizations within the education institution arena, as well as broader cultural norms for education.

2. For instance, teachers in two Michigan high schools told us that declines in the auto industry and increasing unemployment had boosted their general-track students' commitment to school; in this instance, unfavorable local labor market conditions created more favorable working conditions for teachers.

3. We constructed these bridges by replicating survey items from national teacher survey questionnaires in our field survey instruments. For this study, we used the 1984 teacher survey conducted as part of the High School and Beyond (HS&B) program of the National Center for Education Statistics (NCES). Teachers who responded to this survey in 1984 were teaching in schools that were part of a nationally representative sample of U.S. high schools in 1980.

Appendix B

1. See, for example, Education Week, *Quality Counts,* 1997; Firestone, Fuhrman, and Kirst 1989; Lusi 1997.

2. The school board was key in the lives of teachers Willard Waller examined, primarily through the guidelines developed to regulate teachers' personal lives.

3. For example, the fit between teachers' personal values and those of their school has been found to be associated with teachers' commitment to their students and to the profession (Powell 1990). A strong tradition of research highlights the consequences of structural organization and dif-

ferentiation of academic tracks and departments on teachers' conceptions of their work and professional identity (see, for example, Bidwell 1965; Oakes 1985; Sizer 1984; Powell, Farrar, and Cohen 1985; Newmann, Rutter, and Smith 1988).

4. Grant 1988; Hoffer and Coleman 1990; Natriello, McDill, and Pallas 1990.

5. See Natriello, McDill, and Pallas 1990 and Smylie 1994 as examples; see also Anyon 1980 and Metz 1978 for examples of research documenting social class effects on teachers' practice and professional culture.

REFERENCES

Andrew, Michael D. 1990. "Differences between Graduates of Four-Year and Five-Year Teacher Preparation Programs." *Journal of Teacher Education* 41:45–51.

Andrew, Michael D., and Richard L. Schwab. 1995. "Has Reform in Teacher Education Influenced Teacher Performance? An Outcome Assessment of Graduates of an Eleven-University Consortium." *Action in Teacher Education* 17:43–53.

Anyon, Jean. 1980. "Social Class and the Hidden Curriculum of Work." *Journal of Education* 162:67–92.

Apple, Michael. 1982. *Cultural and Economic Reproduction in Education: Essays on Class, Ideology, and the State.* London: Routledge and Kegan Paul.

Ashton, Patricia, and Linda Crocker. 1987. "Systematic Study of Planned Variations: The Essential Focus of Teacher Education Reform." *Journal of Teacher Education* 38:2–8.

Bascia, Nina. 1994. *Unions in Teachers' Professional Lives: Social, Intellectual, and Practical Concerns.* New York: Teachers College Press.

Ball, Deborah L. 1993. With an Eye on the Mathematical Horizon: Dilemmas of Teaching Elementary School Mathematics. *Elementary School Journal* 93:373–97.

Ball, Steven. 1987. *Micropolitics of the School.* London: Methuen; Routledge and Kegan Paul.

Bidwell, Charles E. 1965. "The School as a Formal Organization." In *Handbook of Organizations,* ed. James G. March. Chicago: Rand McNally.

Bransford, John D., Ann L. Brown, and Rodney R. Cocking, eds. 1999. *How people Learn: Brain, Mind, Experience, and School.* Washington, D.C.: National Academy Press.

Brown, Ann, and Joe Campione. 1990. "Communities of Learning and

Thinking, or a Context by Any Other Name." *Human Development* 21:108–25.

———. 1994. "Guided Discovery in a Community of Learners." In *Classroom Lessons: Integrating Cognitive Theory and Classroom Practice,* ed. K. McGilly. Cambridge, MA: MIT Press/Bradford Books.

———. 1996. "Psychological Theory and the Design of Innovative Learning Environments: On Procedures, Principles, and Systems." In *Innovations in Learning: New Environments for Education,* ed. L. Schauble and R. Glaser. Mahwah, N.J.: Erlbaum.

Bruckerhoff, Charles E. 1991. *Between Classes.* New York: Teachers College Press.

Bryk, Anthony S., Valerie E. Lee, and Peter B. Holland. 1993. *Catholic Schools and the Common Good.* Cambridge: Harvard University Press.

Chubb, John E., and Terry M. Moe. 1990. *Politics, Markets, and America's Schools.* Washington, D.C.: Brookings Institution.

Cochran-Smith, Marilyn, and Susan L. Lytle. 1999. "Relationships of Knowledge and Practice: Teacher Learning in Communities." In *Review of Research in Education,* ed. A. Iran-Nejad and C. D. Pearson. Washington: American Educational Research Association.

Cohen, David K., and Heather C. Hill. 1998. *State Policy and Classroom Performance: Mathematics Reform in California.* CPRE Policy Briefs.

———. 2000. "Instructional Policy and Classroom Performance: The Mathematics Reform in California." *Teachers College Record* 102: 294–343.

Cohen, David K., Milbrey W. McLaughlin, and Joan E. Talbert. 1993. *Teaching for Understanding: Challenges for Practice, Research, and Policy.* New York: Jossey-Bass.

Cohen, David K., and James Spillane. 1993. "Policy and Practice: The Relations between Governance and Instruction." In *Designing Coherent Education Policy: Improving the System,* ed. Susan Fuhrman. San Francisco: Jossey-Bass.

Coleman, James S., and Thomas Hoffer. 1987. *Public and Private High Schools: The Impact of Communities.* New York: Basic Books.

Crowson, Robert. 1990. "The Local School District Superintendency, under reform." Editor's introduction to a special issue of the *Peabody Journal of Education* 65:1–8.

Cuban, Larry. 1984. *How Teachers Taught: Constancy and Change in American Classrooms.* New York: Longman.

———. 1990. Reforming Again, Again, and Again. *Educational Researcher* 19:3–13.

Cusick, Philip A. 1973. *Inside High School.* New York: Holt, Rinehart and Winston.

Darling-Hammond, Linda. 1997. *Doing What Matters Most: Investing in*

Quality Teaching. New York: National Commission on Teaching and America's Future.

Darling-Hammond, Linda, and Barnett Berry. 1988. *The Evolution of Teacher Policy.* Santa Monica, Calif.: Rand Corporation; Washington, D.C.: CPRE.

Darling-Hammond, Linda, and Millbrey W. McLaughlin. 1999. "Investing in Teaching as a Learning Profession: Policy Problems and Prospects." In *Teaching as the Learning Profession: Handbook of Policy and Practice,* ed. Linda Darling Hammond and Gary Sykes. San Francisco: Jossey Bass.

Davidson, Ann Locke. 1996. *Making and Molding Identity in Schools: Student Narratives on Race, Gender, and Academic Engagement.* Albany: State University of New York Press.

Davis, Kingsley, and Wilbert E. Moore. 1945. "Some Principles of Stratification." *American Sociological Review* 10:387–94.

Deschenes, Sarah, Larry Cuban, and David Tyack. Forthcoming. "Mismatch: Historical Perspectives on Schools and Students Who Don't Fit Them." *Teachers College Record.*

Eckert, Penelope. 1989. *Jocks and Burnouts: Social Categories and Identity in the High School.* New York: Teachers College, Columbia University.

Edmonds, Ronald. 1979. "Effective Schools for the Urban Poor." *Educational Leadership* 37:15–18, 20–24.

Elmore, Richard. 1993. "The Role of School Districts in Instructional Improvement." In *Designing Coherent Education Policy: Improving the System,* ed. S. H. Fuhrman. San Francisco: Jossey Bass.

Elmore, Richard F., and Milbrey W. McLaughlin. 1988. *Steady Work: Policy, Practice, and the Reform of American Education.* Santa Monica, Calif.: Rand Corporation.

Ferguson, Ronald. 1991. "Paying for Public Education: New Evidence on How and Why Money Matters." *Harvard Journal on Legislation* 28: 465–98.

Fine, Michelle. 1991. *Framing Dropouts: Notes on the Politics of an Urban Public High School.* Albany: State University of New York Press.

Finley, Merrilee. 1984. "Teachers and Tracking in a Comprehensive High School." *Sociology of Education* 57:233–43.

Firestone, William A., Susan H. Fuhrman, and Michael W. Kirst. 1989. *The Progress of Reform: An Appraisal of State Education Initiatives.* New Brunswick, N.J.: Center for Policy Research in Education.

Floden, Robert E. 1988. "Instructional Leadership at the District Level." *Educational Administration Quarterly* 24:96–124.

Fuhrman, Susan, and Jennifer A. O'Day. 1996. *Rewards and Reform: Creating Educational Incentives that Work.* San Francisco: Jossey-Bass.

Fullan, Michael. 1993. *Change Forces: Probing the Depth of Educational Reform.* London: Falmer Press.

Goodlad, John I. 1970. *Behind the Classroom Door.* Worthington, Ohio: C. A. Jones.

Goodson, Ivor. 1983. *School Subjects and Curriculum Change.* London: Croom Helm.

Goodson, Ivor, and Steven Ball, eds. 1984. *Defining the Curriculum: Histories and Ethnographies.* London: Falmer Press.

Greeno, James G., and Shelley V. Goldman. 1998. *Thinking Practices in Mathematics and Science Learning.* Mahwah, N.J.: Lawrence Erlbaum.

Grossman, Pamela L., and Susan S. Stodolsky. 1994. "Considerations of Content and the Circumstances of Secondary School Teaching." In *Review of Research in Education* 20, ed. Linda Darling-Hammond. Washington, D.C: American Educational Research Association.

Grossman, Pamela L., and Susan S. Stodolsky. 1995. "Content as Context: The Role of School Subjects in Secondary School Teaching." *Educational Researcher* 24:5–11.

Grubb, W. Norton. 1995. *Education through Occupations in American High Schools.* New York: Teachers College Press.

Hadley, Martha, and Karen Sheingold. 1993. "Commonalities and Distinctive Patterns in Teachers' Integration of Computers." *American Journal of Education* 101:261–315.

Hargreaves, Andy. 1991. "Contrived Collegiality: The Micropolitics of Teacher Collaboration." In *The Politics of Life in Schools,* ed. J. Blasé. New York: Sage Publications.

———. 1994. *Changing Teachers, Changing Times: Teachers' Work and Culture in the Postmodern Age.* New York: Teachers College Press.

Hawkins, David. 1974. *The Informed Vision: Essays on Learning and Human Nature.* New York: Agathon Press.

Heinz, John P. 1982. *Chicago Lawyers: The Social Structure of the Bar.* New York: Russell Sage Foundation; Chicago: American Bar Foundation.

Hill, Paul T., and Josephine Bonan. 1991. *Decentralization and Accountability in Public Education.* Santa Monica: Rand Corporation.

Huberman, Michael. 1993. *The Lives of Teachers.* New York: Teachers College Press.

Ingersoll, Richard M. 1999. "The Problem of Underqualified Teachers in American Secondary Schools." *Educational Researcher* 28:26–37.

Jackson, Philip W. 1968. *Life in Classrooms.* New York: Teachers College Press.

Johnson, Susan Moore. 1990. *Teachers at Work: Achieving Success in our Schools.* New York: Basic Books.

Kirp, David L., and Donald N. Jensen. 1986. *School Days, Rule Days: The Legalization and Regulation of Education.* London: Falmer Press.

Kozol, Jonathan. 1991. *Savage Inequalities: Children in America's Schools.* New York: Trumpet Club.

Labaree, David F. 1988. *The Making of an American High School.* New Haven: Yale University Press.

Lacey, Colin. 1977. *The Socialization of Teachers.* London: Methuen.

Lave, Jean. 1991. "Situating Learning in Communities of Practice." In *Perspectives on Socially Shared Cognition,* ed. L. Resnick, J. Levine, and S. Teasley. Washington, D.C.: American Psychological Association.

Lave, Jean, and Etienne Wengner. 1991. *Situated Learning: Legitimate Peripheral Participation.* Cambridge: Cambridge University Press.

Lee, Valerie E., and Anthony S. Bryk. 1989. "A Multilevel Model of the Social Distribution of High School Achievement." *Sociology of Education* 62:172–92.

Lieberman, Ann. 1990. *Schools as Collaborative Cultures: Creating the Future Now.* Bristol, Pa: Falmer Press.

Little, Judith Warren. 1982. "Norms of Collegiality and Experimentation: Workplace Conditions of School Success." *American Educational Research Journal* 19:325–40.

———. 1990. "The Persistence of Privacy: Autonomy and Initiative in Teachers' Professional Relations." *Teachers College Record* 91: 509–36.

———. 1993. "Teachers' Professional Development in a Climate of Educational Reform." *Educational Evaluation and Policy Analysis* 15: 129–51.

Little, Judith Warren, and Milbrey W. McLaughlin. 1993. *Teachers' Work: Individuals, Colleagues, and Contexts.* New York: Teachers College Press.

Lord, Brian. 1994. "Teachers' Professional Development: Critical Colleagueship and the Role of Professional Community." In *The Future of Education: Perspectives on National Standards in America,* ed. Norman Cobb. New York: College Entrance Examination Board.

Lortie, Dan C. 1975. *Schoolteacher: A Sociological Study.* Chicago: University of Chicago Press.

———. 1998. "Unfinished work: Reflections on Schoolteacher." In *International Handbook of Educational Change,* eds. Andy Hargreaves, Ann Lieberman, Michael Fullan, and David Hopkins. London: Kluwer Academic Publishers.

Lusi, Susan Follett. 1997. *The Role of State Departments of Education in Complex School Reform.* New York: Teachers College Press.

McDonald, Joseph P. 1992. *Teaching: Making Sense of an Uncertain Craft.* New York: Teachers College Press.

McDonnell, Lorraine M., and Milbrey W. McLaughlin. 1982. *Education Policy and the Role of the States.* Santa Monica: Rand Corporation.

McLaughlin, Milbrey. 1987. "Learning from Experience: Lessons from Policy Implementation." *Educational Evaluation and Policy Analysis* 9:171–78.

McNeil, Linda M. 1986. Contradictions of Control: School Structure and School Knowledge. New York: Routledge and Kegan Paul.

McPherson, Gertrude H. 1972. *Small Town Teacher.* Cambridge: Harvard University Press.

Metz, Mary Haywood. 1978. *Classrooms and Corridors*. Berkeley and Los Angeles: University of California Press.

———. 1986. *Different by Design*. New York: Routledge and Kegan Paul.

———. 1990a. "How Social Class Differences Shape Teachers' Work." In *The Contexts of Teaching in Secondary Schools: Teachers' Realities,* ed. Milbrey McLaughlin, Joan Talbert, and Nina Bascia. New York: Teachers College Press.

———. 1990b. "Real School: A Universal Drama amid Disparate Experience." In *Education Politics for the New Century: The Twentieth Anniversary Yearbook of the Politics of Education Association,* ed. D. Mitchell and M. Goertz. Philadelphia: Falmer Press.

Meyer, John W., and Brian Rowan. 1977. "Institutionalized Organizations: Formal Structure as Myth and Ceremony." *American Journal of Sociology* 83:340–63.

Mortimore, Peter. 1981. *Schools Make a Difference: A Review of the Issues Concerning School-to-College Transition Procedures*. New York: College Board.

Murphy, Jerome.T. 1974. *State Education Agencies and Discretionary Funds*. Lexington, Mass.: Lexington Books.

Murphy, Joseph, and Philip Hallinger. 1988. "Characteristics of Instructionally Effective School Districts." *Journal of Educational Research* 81:175–81.

National Commission on Teaching and America's Future. 1997. *Doing What Matters Most: Investing in Quality Teaching*. New York: National Commission on Teaching and America's Future.

NCES (National Center for Education Statistics). 1996. *Common Core of Data: School Years 1988–89 through 1993–94*. Washington, D.C.: GPO.

Natkins, Lucille G. 1986. *Our Last Term: A Teacher's Diary*. Lanham, Md.: University Press of America.

Natriello, Gary, Edward L. McDill, and Aaron M. Pallas. 1990. *Schooling Disadvantaged Children: Racing against Catastrophe*. New York: Teachers College Press.

Nehring, James. 1989. *Why do we gotta do this stuff, Mr. Nehring? Notes from a Teacher's Day in School*. New York: M. Evans.

Newmann, Fred M., and associates. 1996. *Authentic Achievement: Restructuring Schools for Intellectual Quality*. San Francisco: Jossey Bass.

Nias, Jennifer. 1989. *Primary Teachers Talking: A Study of Teaching as Work*. London: Routledge.

Oakes, Jeannie. 1985. *Keeping Track: How Schools Structure Inequality*. New Haven: Yale University Press.

———. 1990. *Muliplying Inequalities: The Effects of Race, Social Class, and Tracking on Opportunties to Learn in Mathematics and Science*. Santa Monica: Rand Corporation.

———. 1992. "Can Tracking Research Inform Practice? Technical, Normative, and Political Considerations." *Educational Researcher* 21: 12–21.

Page, Reba. 1991. *Lower Track Classrooms: A Curricular and Cultural Perspective.* New York: Teachers College Press.

Parsons, Talcott. 1959. "The School Class as a Social System: Some of Its Functions in American Society." *Harvard Educational Review* 29:297–318.

Perry, Rebecca Reed. 1996. "The Role of Teachers' Professional Communities in the Implementation of California Mathematics Reform." Ph.D. diss., Stanford University.

Phelan, Patricia, Ann L. Davidson, and Hanh Cao Yu. 1998. *Adolescents' Worlds: Negotiating Family, Peers, and School.* New York: Teachers College Press.

Phelan, Patricia, Ann L. Davidson, and Hanh Cao. 1992. "Speaking Up: Students' Perspectives on School." *Phi Delta Kappan* 73.

Powell, Arthur G. 1990. "A Glimpse at Teaching Conditions in Top Private Schools." *American Educator: The Professional Journal of the American Federation of Teachers* 14:28–34, 39.

———. 1996. *Lessons from Privilege: The American Prep School Tradition.* Cambridge: Harvard University Press.

Powell, Arthur G., Eleanor Farrar, and David K. Cohen. 1985. *The Shopping Mall High School: Winners and Losers in the Educational Marketplace.* Boston: Houghton Mifflin.

Ragin, Charles C. 1987. *The Comparative Method: Moving Beyond Qualitative and Quantitative Strategies.* Berkeley and Los Angeles: University of California Press.

Ragin , Charles C., and Howard S. Becker. 1992. *What Is a Case? Exploring the Foundations of Social Inquiry.* Cambridge: Cambridge University Press.

Reed, Deborah, Melissa Glenn Haber, and Laura Mameesh. 1996. *The Distribution of Income in California.* San Francisco: Public Policy Institute of California.

Rosenholtz, Susan J. 1989. *Teachers' Workplace: The Social Organization of Schools.* White Plains: Longman.

Rowan, Brian, Stephen W. Raudenbush, and Yuk Fai Cheong. 1992. "Contextual Effects on the Perceived Self-Efficacy of High School Teachers." *Sociology of Education* 65:150–67.

———. 1993. "Higher Order Instructional Goals in Secondary Schools: Class, Teacher, and School Influences." *American Educational Research Journal* 30:523–53.

Rowan, Brian, Stephen W. Raudenbush, and Sang Jin Kang. 1991. "Organizational Design in High Schools: A Multi-Level Analysis." *American Journal of Education* 99:238–66.

SCANS (The Secretary's Commission on Achieving Necessary Skills). 1992. *Learning a Living: A Blueprint for High Performance.* Washington, D.C.: U.S. Department of Labor.

Schmidt, William, Charles McKnight, and Senta Raizen in collaboration with six others. 1996. *A Splintered Vision: An Investigation of U.S. Science and Mathematics Education, Executive Summary.* Lansing, Mich.: U.S. National Research Center for the Third International Mathematics and Science Study, Michigan State University.

Scott, W. Richard. 1992. *Organizations: Rational, Natural, and Open Systems.* Englewood Cliffs, N.J.: Prentice Hall.

Scott, W. Richard, and John W. Meyer. 1994. *Institutional Environments and Organizations: Structural Complexity and Individualism.* Thousand Oaks, Calif.: Sage Publications.

Senge, Peter M. 1990. *The Fifth Discipline: The Art and Practice of the Learning Organization.* New York: Doubleday/Currency.

Shedd, Joseph B., and Samuel B. Bacharach. 1991. *Tangled Hierarchies: Teachers as Professionals and the Management of Schools.* San Francisco: Jossey-Bass.

Silberman, Charles E. 1964. *Crisis in Black and White.* New York: Random House.

Siskin, Leslie Santee. 1991. "Departments as Different Worlds: Subject Subcultures in Secondary Schools." *Educational Administration Quarterly* 27: 134–60.

———. 1994. *Realms of Knowledge: Academic Departments in Secondary Schools.* Washington, D.C.: Falmer Press.

Siskin, Leslie Santee, and Judith Warren Little. 1995. *The Subjects in Question: Departmental Organization and the High School.* New York: Teachers College Press.

Sizer, Theodore R. 1984. *Horace's Compromise: The Dilemma of the American High School.* Boston: Houghton Mifflin.

Smith, Marshall S., and Jennifer O'Day. 1991. "Systemic School Reform." In *The Politics of Curriculum and Testing,* ed. Susan Fuhrman and Betty Malen. Bristol, Pa.: Falmer Press.

Smylie, Mark A. 1994. "Redesigning Teachers' Work: Connections to the Classroom." In *Review of Research in Education* 20, ed. Linda Darling-Hammond. Washington, D.C.: American Educational Research Association.

Spillane, James P. 1996. "School District Matter: Local Educational Authorities and State Instructional Policy." *Educational Policy* 10:63–87.

Spillane, James P., and Charles L. Thompson. 1997. "Reconstructing Conceptions of Local Capacity: The Local Education Agency's Capacity for Ambitious Instructional Reform." *Educational Evaluation and Policy Analysis* 19:185–203.

Stein, Mary Kay, Edward A. Silver, and Margaret Schwan Smith. 1998. "Mathematics Reform and Teacher Development: A Community of Practice Perspective." In *Thinking Practices in Mathematics and*

Science Learning, ed. J. G. Greeno and S. V. Goldman. Mahwah, N.J.: Lawrence Erlbaum.

Stodolsky, Susan S. 1988. *The Subject Matters: Classroom Activity in Math and Social Studies.* Chicago: University of Chicago Press.

——. 1993. "A Framework for Subject Matter Comparisons in High Schools." *Teaching and Teacher Education* 9:333–46.

Stodolsky, Susan S., and Pamela L. Grossman. 1995. "The Impact of Subject Matter on Curricular Activity: An Analysis of Five Academic Subjects." *American Educational Research Journal* 32:227–49.

Talbert, Joan E. 1986. "The Staging of Teachers' Careers: An Institutional Perspective." *Work and Occupations* 13:421–43.

Talbert, Joan E., with Michele Ennis. 1990. *Teacher Tracking: Exacerbating Inequalities in the High School.* Stanford University: Center for Research on the Context of Teaching.

Talbert, Joan E., and Milbrey W. McLaughlin. 1994. "Teacher Professionalism in Local School Context." *American Journal of Education* 102: 123–53.

Tyack, David. 1974. *The One Best System.* Cambridge: Harvard University Press.

Tyack, David B., and Larry Cuban. 1995. *Tinkering toward Utopia: A Century of Public School Reform.* Cambridge: Harvard University Press, 1995.

Tyack, David, and William Tobin. 1994. "The 'Grammar' of Schooling: Why Has It Been So Hard to Change?" *American Educational Research Journal* 31:453–79.

Tyack, David, Michael Kirst, and Elisabeth Hansot. 1979. *Educational Reform: Retrospect and Prospect.* Stanford: Institute for Research on Educational Finance and Governance.

Viadero, Debra. 1998. "Work vs. Homework." *Education Week* 10.

Waller, Willard. 1932. *The Sociology of Teaching.* New York: John Wiley and Sons.

Weatherley, Richard, and Michael Lipsky. 1977. "Street-Level Bureaucrats and Institutional Innovation: Implementing Special-Education Reform." *Harvard Educational Review* 47:171–97.

Weick, Karl E. 1976. "Educational Organizations as Loosely Coupled Systems." *Administrative Science Quarterly* 21:1–19.

Wenger, Etienne. 1998. *Communities of Practice: Learning, Meaning, and Identity.* Cambridge: Cambridge University Press.

Westheimer, Joel. 1998. *Among Schoolteachers: Community Autonomy and Ideology in Teachers' Work.* New York: Teachers College Press.

Yee, Sylvia Mei-ling. 1990. *Careers in the Classroom: When Teaching Is More Than a Job.* New York: Teachers College Press.

INDEX

Locators in boldface refer to pages with tables or figures.